Girlfriends' Guide to the BIBLE

LATOYA BULLARD-FRANKLIN

GIRLFRIENDS' GUIDE TO THE BIBLE

LATOYA BULLARD-FRANKLIN

Mention of specific companies, organizations, or individuals in this book does not imply endorsements by the author or publisher, nor does mention of specific companies, organizations, or individuals imply they endorse this book, its author, or the publisher.

© 2018 Latoya Bullard-Franklin

All rights reserved. No part of this publication may be reproduced or transmitted in any form or by any means, electronic or mechanical, including photocopying, recording, or any other information storage and retrieval system, without the written permission of the publisher.
Books may be purchased for educational, sales, or promotional use. For requests please contact: Hard Hats & High Heels, 1415 S. Voss Rd., Suite 110-459, Houston, TX 77057, 832-294-9541.
First Edition
All scriptures noted are from the New King James Version of the Holy Bible.
Illustrations and Cover Design by Jerome Vernell, Jr.

ISBN 13: 9780999866207
ISBN-10: 0999866206

For His Grace and Mercy is Sufficient
July 2, 2017

CONTENTS

Letter from the Author ································· ix
The Epiphany ····································· xiii

The Old Testament ································· 1
Chapter 1　Eve: Basic Instinct ······························ 3
　　　　　　Virtue: Love
　　　　　　On the Road Called I-10 ························· 8
Chapter 2　Naamah: Eight is Enough ························ 9
　　　　　　Virtue: "Followship"
Chapter 3　Sarah: Age Ain't Nothing but a Number ············· 21
　　　　　　Virtue: Patience
Chapter 4　Miriam: In God We Trust ······················· 29
　　　　　　Virtue: Trust
　　　　　　On the Road Called I-10: The Rise ················ 36
Chapter 5　Rahab: Roxanne, You Don't Have to Put on the
　　　　　　Red Light ································ 38
　　　　　　Virtue: Faith
Chapter 6　Deborah: Get in Formation ······················ 48
　　　　　　Virtue: Leadership

Chapter 7	Ruth: Widow's Peak · 57	
	Virtue: Loyalty	
Chapter 8	Esther: Hidden in Plain Sight· 66	
	Virtue: Courage	
	On the Road Called I-10: The Reason · · · · · · · · · · · · · · · · 73	

The New Testament · 77

Chapter 9	Mary: We'll Leave the Light on for You · · · · · · · · · · · · · · 79	
	Virtue: Acceptance	
Chapter 10	Samaritan Woman: Past-Perfect Tense · · · · · · · · · · · · · · · · 88	
	Virtue: Perseverance	
Chapter 11	Mary and Martha: Mary Don't You Weep; Martha,	
	Put Those Dishes Down! · 95	
	Virtue: Worship	
	On the Road Called I-10: The Rebirth · · · · · · · · · · · · · · · 102	
Chapter 12	Mary Magdalene: Great Expectations · · · · · · · · · · · · · · · 104	
	Virtue: Belief	

Prayer: Our Conversations with God· · · · · · · · · · · · · · · · 117
Women of the Bible· 119
References · 121
Dedication · 123

LETTER FROM THE AUTHOR

To all my sisters, I say welcome. To my Christian, Jewish, Hindu, and Buddhist sisters, welcome. To all wives, mothers, daughters, queens, woman warriors, entrepreneurs, STEM pursuers, innovators, and educators, I say welcome. To my cooks, bakers, candlestick makers, my nose wipers, my changers of the diapers, my CEO women, my "I got it, I already know" women, boss ladies, bag ladies, and every destiny chaser in between, welcome to you!

Welcome to the *Girlfriends' Guide to the Bible*. I will be your host along our journey through biblical stories that have been told for ages. We will view them through new, rose-colored glasses to explore the positive impact of women in establishing the Bible as the bestseller of all time. *National Geographic* recently released a publication of the fifty most influential people of the Bible, and although the magazine prominently displayed many women in this list of fifty, it was the characterization of the Bible that was a bit disappointing. The publication stated the following regarding the Bible: "At first, the scope of the book is universal…soon, however, the narrative narrows down to a series of patriarchal stories." This is the focus of many of the stories of the Bible—they are primarily patriarchal. Along our journey, we will uncover the great matriarchs that lie within these stories, and we'll discover the great matriarch that lies within you.

My welcome of the myriad of roles we serve is purposeful because within our "sister circle," we are all every-woman. Oftentimes we are each asked to be every-woman all at the same time. Suddenly, our questions abound: How do we do it all with the least collateral damage to our minds, bodies, and spirits? How do we make significant impacts in our families, neighborhoods, and communities despite unbalanced gender expectations? How do we succeed and grow in our male-dominated day?

This book will answer these questions and more through the voices of virtuous women in the Bible. They braved the gender divide to stand up and be counted at a time when, culturally, women were to be seen and not heard.

Today, we can be seen as well as heard, but the World Economic Forum states that we will not arrive at economic and social equality of the sexes for another 177 years. In America, this is projected to happen in 2058, which is an improvement, but it is still terribly slow. It's a tad bit frustrating, isn't it? It's okay to be angry, but let's channel that energy into being productive. A great woman once said, "There is no point in blaming the men; we made them!"

The beautiful women of the Bible give us tips on just how to do that. It is amazing how the most forgotten-about women of the Bible—those who were the most discarded and disregarded during their time—made the greatest impacts on the history of our biblical teachings. This is because He Who is within us is Whom everyone should see. Our light comes from the illumination of the Word inside of us. It is a fact that light can only shine through a vessel that is broken. Time and time again, God chose women who were broken through which to shine His light the brightest.

The Samaritan woman with five ex-husbands, who was living with a man who was not her husband, became the evangelist to the Gentiles of Samaria to spread the Good News. Rahab was a prostitute who then became the key to the Israelites possessing their promised land and became part of the lineage of Jesus. Mary Magdalene, who was demon possessed and was once believed to be a harlot, set the foundation for what Christianity is today.

We should find encouragement in the lives of these biblical women—encouragement that even with brokenness, we can still be used to bring glory to this earth. Just as the Japanese art form of Kintsugi believes, all the broken pieces makes us uniquely qualified to make a positive impact on the world. We will explore the virtues that these women exhibited in the face of all odds and attempt to find comfort in their stories of triumph and perseverance.

Grab your Bible, your pen, and your passport journal as we embark upon an expedition of transformational growth together!

Sisterly,
Latoya Bullard-Franklin

THE EPIPHANY

As a little girl growing up, I was pretty much in church every day that ended in the letter *y*. All those years of being an active participant in church encouraged me to see the Bible as a behemoth—a monstrous book that could only be conquered by pastors, deacons, and bishops. (And oh, by the way, female biblical scholars need not apply.)

Every Sunday I listened to ministers quote scriptures and provide context to the stories outlined in the Bible. Along with the rest of the female members of the congregation, I was urged to attend Bible study, serve on youth committees, and ultimately become a member of the all-female missionary society. Even after serving valiantly for years, I still felt that something was missing. I wanted more, so I sought out further enlightenment by enrolling in Bible and religion courses in college in hopes of filling the void.

I soon had an epiphany and realized that I was pursuing religion and not my relationship with God. So I redirected my path in my quest for a relationship with Him by reading the Bible—this time with the intent to understand.

As I began my quest for knowledge, I uncovered answers to many of life's questions. I've always had a keen curiosity to know and honor those queens of my ancestry who came before me. I've been interested in knowing why I think the way that I think. Why do I move the way that I move? Why do I feel the way that I feel? Did they experience life the same way that I have? What's in my DNA? Finding answers to these questions has brought me great comfort and has fed my soul.

I've found comfort in getting answers and direction from women like Rahab, Deborah, and Esther. These women have become my "biblical sister circle." Finally, the reason why I am so intrigued with the women of the Bible is clear. It peaks the same curiosity; it feeds the soul just the same. These women are a part of my ancestry; we are all descendants of Eve and thus all from the same family.

Just as I would confide in, and find consolation through life's troubles with, my girlfriends in daily life, these biblical girlfriends provided me with guidance as their experiences were similar to mine. The women I encountered are important fabrics in the beautiful tapestry that is the Bible.

The biblical stories of obedience, leadership, and loyalty are true blueprints for life. With their help, I've discovered how to navigate life with better precision and focus. As I dug deeper into the traditional stories of Moses, David, and Jesus, I found women of triumph, women of courage, and women of integrity. They were there all along, and they even exemplify the saying, "Behind every great man, there is an *even greater* woman." (Yes, I did change it up a bit!)

We are all daughters of Eve, and it doesn't matter in which religion you believe or with which denomination you identify. These are stories of heroism, of women who came before us, and of the lessons from their journeys in the past that are relevant to our journeys today.

THE OLD TESTAMENT

Chapter 1
BASIC INSTINCT

EVE

BIBLE READING: GENESIS 1–3
VIRTUE: LOVE

Dear Daughter,

Over the years, women have experienced difficulties getting this male-female-relationship thing right. I come to offer insight into how to get and keep things on track and in alignment with God's plan. But first, let me provide a bit of background. The Creator had just completed a marathon run of creating the solar system, heaven and earth, and all living things. He took a step back to survey the landscape and felt a sense of pride for what He had accomplished—as He should have, because this was quite the feat. But then He thought, "There is one piece missing."

That piece was my handsome, strong, amazing Adam. You see, God needed some hands on deck to rule over and manage earth so that He could continue to rule from heaven. Adam was proud to be called God's best creation. After all, it is quite an honor to be called the best in comparison to the entire galaxy!

God realized He had created both male and female for the beasts of the field and the fowl of the air. Adam needed a mate as well. Adam's loneliness was obvious, and God decided to help a brother out. So he performed the first anesthesia treatment in history, putting Adam to sleep and taking not a hair from his head nor a toe from his foot, but a rib from his side to create me. This was an important and symbolic move on God's part. A body part was not selected from the top or bottom to designate either an upper- or lower-level position to Adam but from the side to denote that we should always strive to walk side by side with our men.

Adam and I were enjoying life, living footloose and fancy free, a kind of Bonnie-and-Clyde dream, the good life. But I was always curious about the tree of good and evil. I would ask Adam about it, and he kept telling me not to think about it because God said it was not for us to partake of for now. There were thousands of other trees God had blessed us with, but there was something about that one tree.

The evil one saw a prime opportunity to push my curiosity into the land of no return, making me feel as if I had to do something. It never occurred to me that in all of His creating, God would devise an evil element. I guess the old saying is true that "curiosity killed the cat."

Only when it was too late did I realize that God is all about balance. In His first creation of light, He also created darkness. And as He created the animals, He created the circle of life. So it was when He created Adam and me; He created the antithesis evil one as a foil to the human race.

This is important—never give the evil one too much power. The evil one was created by God, so he will never be God's equal. Ask yourself—how can something be equal to its creator? You should never assume that he is on the same level as a decision to go with God. And this was my tragic mistake, my fatal flaw. By partaking of the tree of good and evil, I equated following the evil one as comparable to obeying God. In the process, I got in the way of my man's blessings just as so many other women after me will do, like my sister Sarah.

I never thought such a small decision to eat a fruit would bear so much burden for women to carry for the rest of humanity. Latoya, please accept my sincerest apologies for that childbirth thing! If I had known what I know now, I wouldn't have taken the evil one's option. Instead of offering Adam an alternate solution, which I mistakenly thought would help him, I should have just offered him the only solution: continued trust in God.

Sincerely,
Eve

THE GIVE-RECEIVE MODEL

So it all began with Eve—the struggles, strife, and entry of sin into this world. She was certainly the Bonnie to Adam's Clyde. And if we are really honest with ourselves, she was the mastermind behind the whole ordeal. Like Eve, I think most of us would have made a similar decision if approached by the evil one. (Throughout the course of this book, I will not give a proper name to "he who shall not be named" because speaking his name would give him power. When we say things such as "the devil made me do it" or "the devil sure is busy," we give him power. The enemy is absolutely powerless. He only gains power in your life when you give it to him.) If we believe that God our Father is all-powerful, those types of statements should never enter our minds, leave our lips, or be allowed to enter our atmosphere.

She and Adam were birthed into a perfect world as perfect human beings. It was a perfect world without blemish. This perfection is directly correlated with complete trust in God. Eve was a willing participant in ushering imperfection into this world. Perfection is created from absolute trust in God, and anything less leads to imperfection. The sin stain she created was irremovable; the choice she made was irrevocable. Her basic instinct was her fatal flaw.

Evil came to her with an option to directly betray the only rule God gave to them: not to partake of the fruit from the tree of life. Eve's basic instinct as a nurturer was to help Adam to be the best man he could be.

Unfortunately, her decision led her to not trust God, but to trust evil instead. This laid the groundwork for the angst we experience today in platonic relationships and marriage. Instead of offering Adam *her* solution, she should have offered him *the* solution—to trust in God.

Eve thought her decision to take the evil one's offer was the best way to show love to him. She wanted him to have all the knowledge he could get—and right away. The story of Adam and Eve shows how much power we have over our men, and it is the first example of a man being persuaded by feminine wiles. Through love, we have a great deal of power. But unfortunately, and more often than not, we misuse and abuse that power. In our earnest attempts to help, it is like we are micromanaging God's blessings. The only guidance we should provide our men is to encourage them to trust in God. Ladies, we need to learn to pray, obey, and get out of the way! Pray to God on his behalf, and ask that He anoint him with the direction in alignment with His will. Obey the actions God gives us through prayer, and then get out of the way and let God have His way. Any other direction merely guides our men into sin's trap.

I've seen this go awry in single-parent and absentee-father homes where mothers overcompensate for the lack of male role models by over-nurturing their sons. They give their sons anything and everything they want. Although this giving comes from a place of love, it reinforces an unbalanced level of trust for women over God. This sets the foundation for unbalanced expectations in future adult relationships and marriage.

According to the 2016 US Census Bureau, nearly 80 percent of the eleven million single-parent households are headed by single mothers. With more than one child in many of these households, this equates to 17.2 million children being raised without fathers. Our Adams develop so much trust in women that when they find their Eves, they expect them to give, give, and give as their mothers did. Instead, the expectation should be that their Eves will receive, receive, and receive the blessings God bestows upon them as a couple through him as the man.

The Give-Receive model established by God is this:

> God gives to man. Man trusts God. Man receives his blessings and protection from the evil one in the Spirit. Man gives the blessings and protection to the woman in the natural. The woman receives and proceeds to replenish earth with her light and reciprocates this love to the man. This gives man strength and power to continually trust in God.

This circle of life was broken by Eve, and now we as women have to continue to replace and reconnect this chain to bring harmony back into our lives. With hard work and dedication, the proper balance can be achieved. Eve, your Eden is out there!

ENCOURAGEMENT EXERCISE: THE SOLUTION

At the end of each chapter, I will introduce an exercise of encouragement. It is my hope that these suggested exercises will bring about a greater you and a renewed sense of self in connection with the Bible.

Over the next week, make a conscious effort to lead your spouse to seek God's face, listen to His guidance, and trust and obey His Word. When your spouse or significant other comes to you with a problem, don't offer him your solution. Instead, offer him *the* solution: trust in God. Keep a tally of the number of times in which your first instinct is to offer him your solution. Over the next three months, your goal is to keep track of your daily tally and hopefully reduce this number to zero.

Some of you may say, "Latoya, I'm not currently in a relationship, so this doesn't apply to me." Yes, it still does. As a mother, you can apply this exercise in your interactions with your son. As a sister, you can apply this exercise with your brother. This will help to prepare you for your Adam who is sure to come.

ON THE ROAD CALLED I-10

On the road called I-10 is where it all begins,
the only pathway where change for me happens.
I experience a life shift,
an encounter with Him as God's gift.
Each encounter, more precious than the last,
renews my strength and redirects where my gaze is cast,
continually on Him as my source for light, power, and strength;
my life's path cemented in the infinite.

Interstate 10 (I-10) is a major highway that spans the Southern United States from Jacksonville, Florida, to Santa Monica, California. In total, it is 2,460 miles, providing plenty of time for reflection while traversing such a broad expanse. I am most familiar with the stretches from Houston to Baton Rouge to New Orleans.

It is on I-10 where I am most inspired. His purpose for me is revealed, and I always encounter a significant life change. Throughout this book, you'll see pieces of "On the Road Called I-10." It's the glue that pulls it all together for me. Along the road, I have plenty of time to listen to my innermost thoughts and actually make sound decisions. The forks in the road that I approach are direct metaphors for my life at various times. It is my hope that my journey on I-10 will lead you to find the common thread of revelation in your own life as well.

Chapter 2
EIGHT IS ENOUGH

NAAMAH

BIBLE READING: GENESIS 6–9

VIRTUE: "FOLLOWSHIP"

Dear Latoya,

Phew, we made it! We both made it through a treacherous storm that seemed like it would never end. And we both made it through by following God's Word–God's Word conveniently sent through our earthly protectors, our husbands. I can remember it like it was yesterday. Noah came to me to deliver the instructions that God had given to him. It was quite the undertaking and definitely a head-scratcher.

As Noah walked away, I was left with more questions than answers. "You have to build what by yourself? This ark thing has to be how large? And why can't you ask our neighbors for help? Why can't we bring them onto the ark to seek refuge?" As the questions continued to leave my lips, I eventually realized that I was being more of a nagging wife than a supportive one. So I stopped with the inquisition. I closed my lips in order to open my heart to God in prayer. It was at this time that the answers to my questions began to enter my spirit. He responded with saying, "I am the Lord thy God, Maker of heaven and earth." In a nutshell, He was saying to me, "Because I said so!"

I wanted to take my best friend and her family as well as my best material possessions, for crying out loud. But Noah continued to veto my requests. He said no because they were not the specific instructions the Lord had given to him. At first, it was difficult for me to understand that God would not want us to place more people on the ark to save as many as we possibly could. God is love, and if I didn't extend a helping hand, I felt that I was not loving others and thus not serving Him. But then I prayed to God for comfort and understanding. He assured me that Noah's direction to me was indeed His direction to him, and I should simply follow Noah's lead. His sovereign answer was good enough for me.

I know from your experience enduring Hurricane Harvey that you went through the same level of inquisition from others that I went through. A million and one inquiries: "What is he doing? Has your husband gone mad? Are you sure he's following God?" You and I also experienced fear of the unknown. This fear manifested into tears—tears of loss as we grieved for the losses that we knew were inevitable. Tears because at that time, when the storm was raging, there was seemingly no end in sight. The homes where we raised our families would be gone. As the sun would rise for a new day, we would look out of the window for a sign that the storm was over. We then would breathe sighs of relief that our families were spared to see the light of day. But we also felt despair and exhausted that the storm still raged on. When would it all end?

As I looked over at Noah, he remained at peace; nary a hair was out of place. At times I became frustrated that his hair was not standing on end like mine. Why wasn't he experiencing the same yo-yo of emotions as me? The Lord calmed my spirit and helped me to understand that Noah was called to be the protector for our family. As our protector, he was given specific instructions from God on how to protect. In order to make it through the *storm and reach our new beginnings, I must simply follow. If we follow His lead, God will supply all our needs.*

Sincerely,
Naamah

THE LEADER

God was displeased with humankind, and He searched high and low for one great person that He could use as His "boots on the ground." Because Noah walked with God, He chose Noah for His great act of recharging mankind. He was very specific to Noah on His instructions for the building of the ark, His timing of the storm, and who would be allowed on the ark. I'm pretty sure that there were many comments and suggestions from others to deter Noah from the plan that God gave him. There were most certainly pleas from his wife to include others on the ark, because as women, our instincts are to nurture. But Noah was very clear in executing the vision that God had given to him. Noah was in total obedience to God and did all that God commanded him (Genesis 6:22). And his wife followed his lead because of the words that God had spoken to him.

At the start of Hurricane Harvey, all reports indicated that once the storm hit land, the bulk of the damage would be centered seventy miles or more from my home. I walked around with my head held high, thinking, "I'm from New Orleans. I've experienced massive storms before. I can do this."

I'm well equipped to deal with these high-pressure situations. I usually know what to do, how to do it, and when to do it. With serving in lead roles in my business, church, or the community, I am always required to step up and make all of the decisions. I'm like many of you; as type-A women, our confidence in navigating high-pressure situations successfully can often lead to unintended consequences in our relationships. We can sometimes become adversarial with our significant others, thinking we have all the right answers and can do it all on our own. Instead, we should be holding onto each other. Otherwise the evil one will try to use the raging winds and rain to cause division and defeat. The metaphorical storm can break us apart. But this is the time when it is most critical for couples to stay in alignment with God's purpose and with the Give-Receive model. When balance is achieved, the blessings from God to weather the storm will be received.

As the storm raged on, I became increasingly concerned. To cope, I joked with family and friends that we were figuratively on the ark, and we must have been in for forty days just like Noah and his family. At first I couldn't understand my husband's decision not to evacuate because everyone else nearby was doing so as a precaution. Then, we received the evacuation orders for our neighborhood, confirming that staying in our home was the right decision.

On the evacuation map, there was a thin triangle of white in a sea of red. As I zoomed in, I could see that this thin, white triangular area was deemed a safe zone not requiring evacuation. In this safe zone, there was only one main street that ran through; it was my street. I shouted, "Hallelujah!" to God and then immediately ran to tell my husband the great news.

Surely this was the signal to invite anyone and everyone we could to safety in our home, our ark. Initially, I couldn't understand why my husband's response was that I shouldn't invite everyone to come over. I went to my prayer closet to pray to God and thank Him for providing safety and to ask Him for answers. God's response was to clarify the roles and responsibilities of my husband and me. His response to me was simple: in order to keep us in perfect peace as the storm raged outside our doors, I must accept my husband's role to give protection to the household and receive direction and vision from God. My role is to set the atmosphere, spread light, and receive and trust in my husband's guidance as he trusts in the Lord. I had an epiphany, and immediately a sense of peace came over my spirit. I finally realized that exhibiting "followship" allowed a weight to be lifted from my shoulders. I didn't have to figure it all out on my own and do it all on my own. I had a partner who would lead me to safety through the physical storms as well as the metaphorical storms in my life.

So I began to offer up intercessory prayers of protection for my family and friends, and I anointed our home with oil throughout. I exhibited followship, and God kept us in perfect peace as the storm raged outside our doors. Through this experience, I learned that following my husband is not about losing my voice but about finding my voice with God. As a wife, I must trust in God and obey His Word that He often will give to my husband. I will continue to pray to God concerning my husband, intervening on his behalf so that he stays in alignment with God's Word. Only when we learn to follow will we be able to truly lead in His kingdom.

THE NUMBERS

The number eight signifies new beginnings. It was purposeful because God told Noah and Naamah that eight was enough. He only asked Noah to bring immediate family and didn't ask him to bring cousins, in-laws, or other males. God was purposeful in bringing an equal number of males and females onto the ark as a symbol for God's promise of new beginnings. Perhaps with God asking them to only bring their immediate family, He wanted to show us the importance we should place on our immediate family. After forty days, the storm was over, and the waters ceased. The ark rested on the highest mountaintop of Ararat in the seventh month, on the seventeenth day of the month. Noah first sent a raven to fly high and then a dove in two seven-day increments to fly low to ascertain whether it was safe to disembark from the ark. The dove brought back an olive branch to signify that the waters had receded and the trees were viable for food again. Even when he knew the coast was clear, he still waited before exiting the ark. He waited until God spoke to him and instructed him to do so. This is why olive branches and doves are symbols of peace and signify the ends of adverse events to this day.

The forty days of the storm correlated to the four hundred years of enslavement in Egypt that God prophesized to Abraham and the forty years in the wilderness before reaching the promise (Genesis 15:13–16). Even after the storm was complete, there still were more trials and more storms to endure before reaching the promise. The fluent use of numbers was deliberate and essential in the storytelling of God's covenant with mankind through Noah and Naamah.

* Eight: God only allowed eight people on the ark to begin humanity again.
* Seven: Noah waited seven days after the dove brought back an olive branch to ensure that it didn't return again. Once the dove didn't return, he knew the coast was clear to begin unloading the ark.
* Six: Noah was six centuries old at the time of the flood.
* Five: After the waters receded, five months later, the boat came to rest on Mt. Ararat.
* Four: The number of seasons that God said would remain—seedtime and harvest, winter and summer.
* Three: God instructed Noah to create three decks on the ark—a lower deck, a second deck, and a third deck.
* Two: Two birds were sent out to confirm that the storm was over. The first was a raven, which typically flies high, to assess whether the water had receded in the high areas. The second was a dove, which typically flies low in valleys.
* One: God revealed a rainbow in the clouds to seal His promise that He would never destroy the earth by water again.

THE WATER

Water is such an extraordinary force, and it is the perfect resource to show that we serve an extraordinary God. The same force that is so critical to sustaining life, however, has the ability to end it as well. Water from the Euphrates and Tigris rivers provided the life force to the cradle of civilization. This is the same water that also served as an agent of death during the 2011 tsunami in Japan that claimed the lives of more than fifteen thousand people. Because of this duality, God used water to establish His first covenant with humankind.

Living in Houston, when we first received the forecast for Hurricane Harvey, I was confident and optimistic. Even though it hovered over the Gulf of Mexico for quite a while, by the time it was scheduled to reach land, it was only supposed to be a category 1 storm with winds at 75 mph at best. So I walked around with my head held high, purchased the items necessary to hunker down, and prepared for my "hurricane party." Yes, you read that correctly: a party for a hurricane. You may be thinking, "A party? During a time in which a major storm is looming, how can anyone think of hosting a party?" But being a New Orleans native, I can attest that this was quite the norm for us. As New Orleanians, we became so immune to the cycle of tropical storms, flash floods, and hurricanes. We found that the best way to cope was to "ride out" the storm with family and friends.

My family members would pull out their best recipes to cook the massive amounts of food they had just purchased from the crowded stores. We sat around the television or the radio to listen to the updates in weather reports. In between the time of the reports, we played board games or cards, danced, laughed, and enjoyed each other's company. Ironically, torrential storms produced some of the fondest memories of our childhoods, and we embraced the idea of an approaching storm due to its ability to slow things down for us and reconnect with our loved ones—that is, until Hurricane Katrina occurred.

Hurricane Katrina was a devastating force, and the emotional, financial, and psychological tolls that it took on those from my native city is immeasurable. Its impact on the American landscape is far-reaching too, in that the displacement of New Orleanians has now created enclaves of Creole culture across the country. I'm curious to see the results of studies that will be conducted some twenty or thirty years post-Katrina on the cultural impact that it had on cities across America.

Although I was living in Boston at the time of Hurricane Katrina, I was still personally impacted. My family and friends who still resided in New Orleans were devastated and displaced. I went to sleep one evening at peace because I had spoken to my family; they had all successfully and safely evacuated. Then I was shocked to awaken the next morning to hear news that the city was not. The storm produced a deluge of water that was too powerful for the levee system to bear. The floodwaters caused widespread destruction immediately across the city.

As soon as I arrived at work, I sat at my office computer and tuned in to view what was happening online. I was in total disbelief of the reports I was receiving, so I just had to see for myself. I was heartbroken as I watched streets, buildings, and locations that I had frequented become demolished. My memories had washed away, and I wept heavily for my city, for the city I had once known would be no more. My range of emotions was vast. I was sad and worried as I tried to account for the whereabouts of family members and friends. I was angry because I felt that more should have been done to protect the city from such immense destruction by water. I was determined to uncover what more could have been done. As an engineer, I felt that more should have been done to assess and manage the risks of a levee-system breach that could ultimately destroy the city. But most of all, I was optimistic. If God allowed it to pass, then it would be for the good of my city. Maybe God was using this flooding as a wake-up call. Maybe God was using the water as a spiritual cleansing. Whatever His reasoning, it will never be known to us for sure. But what was known is that God would ensure that New Orleans would rise once again—brighter and better than ever before.

THE STORM

One of my husband's favorite sayings is that at any point in time, every individual is in either one of three phases in his or her life. Either you are (1) about to enter a storm; (2) in a storm; or (3) just about to come out of a storm. He likes this phrase so much that he put it on a T-shirt! Storms in life are truly inevitable, so metaphorically they serve as a common ground for us to experience as human beings. It's all about the process and how we manage through the process that will make us or break us. The sizes of the storms will be analogous to our destinies. The bigger the storm, the greater the blessing He has in store for us. When the storm starts, sometimes it's just light rain, so we say, "Let me just get my cute umbrella," and then we begin singing in the rain. For us from New Orleans, we may even begin our own second-line parades.

Then, the storm gets a little crazier, the rain rages a bit harder, and we look up at God and say "Really?" Now we are forced to go back inside to get our hooded raincoats, because God forbid we mess up the hair. (We've just spent $100 and endured five hours at the salon to capture just the right look.) We look up at God and ask, "Now God, I know you don't want me to waste my money on this hairdo. I've paid my tithe; now what else is a girl to do?"

God's response is to pump up the volume and send the wind and a torrential downpour, so next, we grab our galoshes. Then here comes the hail, and we've never seen hail this size before. That's when we begin to feel very uneasy and unsure, because the sky is falling. We continue to look to the sky for answers, and we quickly become reincarnations of the spirit of Job and ask, "Why? But God, you said you would" (Job 7:20–21). In this moment, perfect storms are raging in our lives, and these moments are the most critical. It is important that we tap into our relationships with God in order to endure. It's all about the intonation and the inflection in our voices when we exclaim, "But, God!" We need to transform our "But Goooooooodddddddddd!" from a whiny tone into "But! God!" to signify triumph.

"But God, I was going through the worst year in my life. I lost my mom, I lost my job, and I lost my sanity. But! God! God is in control!"

"My child is running amok, and my husband is running the streets, But! God!"

It is with this simple declaration that we remember we have all the protection we need in our closets, our whole armor of God (Ephesians 6:11–17). We trust that God will always be our protector and provider to sustain us through whatever storms may come. We remember that God's got our back, and we cast all of our cares on Him. Then God will shout "Peace be still!" and the winds and the waters will cease (Mark 4:37–39). And just like that, the storm is over. There is a moment of breakthrough, and He breaks every chain. We see a rainbow peak through the clouds, a signal that the worst has passed, and a new journey on a new path has begun.

Storms are inevitable, and they will come. You can't control the storm, but the only thing you can control is your perspective. I always look at the storm as a cleansing and determine what God is trying to strip from me so that I'm lighter and freer to pursue my destiny. I determine what lesson He wishes for me to learn and place in my arsenal so I am armed and ready for greatness. No matter how great the storm is, I will be victorious. After the forty days of the biblical storm, God rested Noah and the ark on Mt. Ararat, the highest mountain. The Lord will also do the same for us, resting us at greater heights than we've ever experienced before.

WHO'S THAT LADY?

Noah's wife was never called by name in the Bible; however, biblical scholars have three names that they have found for her. She was a descendant of Cain and was called Naamah, Emzara, or Barthenos. Naamah is the most widely used and translates to "beautiful or pleasant one."

ENCOURAGEMENT EXERCISE: MINIMIZE YOUR LIFE TO MAXIMIZE YOUR WALK

During Hurricane Harvey, I was provided with my real-life Noah's-ark situation. In the aftermath, I entered into a period of reflection and asked myself when it was time to evacuate, what did I feel was important to place in that one large suitcase? As I assessed the items that were in my home that remained unaffected by the storm, I wondered, "Why do I have all of this stuff?" I felt a bit ashamed, especially when there are people who had lost all of their earthly possessions. Basically, at the most critical time, what was most important for me to protect?

In the average American home, there are approximately three hundred thousand items, most of which will go untouched, unseen, and unutilized within a calendar year. Every year, not only do we not purge these items, but we compound the problem by bringing in more stuff that is placed on top of and in front of the old stuff until it becomes an astronomical force that becomes too overwhelming to handle. In conversations with my girlfriends, I found that many of us were experiencing this same existential crisis. We were reflective as a result of the storm, wondering how we can minimize the stuff in our lives—the stuff that we have held onto for some hypothetical scenarios in the future that would never come to fruition. We think this stuff brings us a sense of comfort. But if we are not using it in the present, the only thing we are doing is holding on to the past. My thoughts are that this excess stuff can be a direct factor in keeping us bound to the past and incapable of moving forward to the promise that God has before us.

As destiny would have it, my dear friend invited me to a talk hosted by these two gentlemen who call themselves "The Minimalists." Their goal is to assist people with pursuing minimalist lifestyles and with ridding themselves of excess items in their personal spaces that can lead to excess clutter in their lives as well as their minds. After this engaging talk, a group of four of us decided to place one of their exercises into action: the thirty-day challenge. We served as accountability partners for each other, and every day via group text, we would send pictures of progress. It was such a gratifying process for us all, and we were able to enjoy wonderful results.

My encouragement to you is to complete this thirty-day challenge as well. It is a very creative and productive way to declutter your life. For each day of the month, remove the number of items from your home that correspond to the date. You can decide to discard, recycle, donate, or even sell these items online or during a garage sale. The only rule is that these items must leave your space. For example, for day one, remove one item from your home; on day two, remove two items from your home, and so on and so forth until you arrive at day thirty and remove thirty items from your home on that day. At the end of the month, you will be able to remove 465 items from your life. Happy hunting!

Chapter 3

AGE AIN'T NOTHING BUT A NUMBER

SARAH

BIBLE READING: GENESIS 11–23
VIRTUE: PATIENCE

Dear Brittanie,

I've watched over you as you have braved the journey to become a mother. Your courage, perseverance, and tenacity are to be applauded. Your tear-soaked pillows represent your battle scars, and crying out to the Lord asking Him, "Why?" became your battle cry. Trust me, I totally understand your heartache and pain. I encourage you to stay focused on God's promise for you. Your destiny is unfolding right before your eyes. I want you to be at peace in knowing that God has already allowed you to become a mother and to give birth to a great promise—your hair salon. God is so very proud of you for nurturing and carrying His promise to term. He sees your continual sacrifice and your giving heart in raising your promise to be the beautiful daughter she is today.

Through your nurturing, the salon has become the epicenter of love and a safe haven for many women. This, daughter, was called impossible by many. But I'm so glad we serve the God of the impossible. Your giving birth to this promise before the age of thirty is proof positive of God's promise to bring the impossible to pass. So calm your fears and dry your tears because nothing is too large or too impossible for God to transition to the possible on this earth.

I come to you to give you a word of advice because I see such similarities in our journeys. I had to learn the hard way. P-A-T-I-E-N-C-E will set you free! God will always give you what He has promised you. He is a faithful God, and He always delivers on time, His time. Exhibiting patience gives you the freedom to enjoy the life God has given you at the moment, a sense of peace that your past has greater purpose. You will be open to receive the blessings He has in store for you in the present.

I couldn't and wouldn't for the life of me embrace patience. When Abraham and I arrived at Canaan with our caravan in tow, God gave him the promise that he would be the father of many nations, with his descendants as numerous as the stars. I was sixty-six, and he was seventy-five. I would hardly call that childbearing age. I knew God had given Abraham a promise to be the father of His chosen people. But I thought that I could help to make it possible right now. I thought that if I hadn't given birth at my age, then it would probably never happen. I believed that Hagar was a more suitable candidate to provide Abraham with this much-needed heir. So she bore him a son, and I was terribly unhappy. I thought that I would be happy in helping my husband reach his destiny. But I felt mostly contempt because this drove a wedge between us—a wedge of blood with which I couldn't compete. If only I had held my peace and waited on the Lord.

Then, some years later, He sent His angels to our camp to tell Abraham that I would indeed still bear him a son. I was eavesdropping, as any good wife would do when strangers come to her home. I laughed when I heard the news. And it was a good laugh too. It felt good to laugh like that since I hadn't in a while. I was ninety years old, for crying out loud! Then God called me on it, and I was so embarrassed, so I just lied and said that I hadn't laughed. God's response to me was this: "I see all and hear all. Girl, you did laugh!" I was still in disbelief. How can I carry a child at my age? What will the women say? I thought they would laugh at me and say, "Girl, you are way too old. You don't know nothing about birthing a baby!"

Even in my disbelief, God still found us and blessed Abraham and me together. I gave birth to my beautiful baby boy Isaac a year later, and this is what set God's plan in motion for His chosen people. And that's the beauty of serving a mighty God, He will find you and deliver the blessing you need, just in time and right on time. Just like the woman who battled with the blood infirmity for eighteen years.

For over eighteen years, she'd tried all the best doctors around, and not one could heal her. But as soon as He was ready, Jesus found her and healed her. That is just how God works; His blessing can come in an instant. What may have been seen as a lifetime of suffering was like eighteen seconds to Him. I got in God's way and tried to fix things because I was anxious for His blessing. My impatience got the best of me because I thought surely, He had forgotten about me.

My dear sister, just when you think God has forgotten about His promise to you, He will find you. If He said He would do it, it will come to pass. I'll leave you with the words from Lauryn Hill to keep you encouraged as you patiently await God's blessing:

"Everything is everything. What is meant to be will be. After winter must come spring. Change, it comes eventually."

Sincerely,
Sarah

JUST-IN-TIME DELIVERY

What we learn from Sarah's life is that God never forgets His promise to you. If God said it, it will most surely come to pass. The thing that looks dead can still be resurrected just as Lazarus was (John 11). He has the power to complete the vision He has given to you. You must hold on to your faith even when the situation seems dead and done for in the natural. In the spirit, He will not only resurrect the possibility but also bring it to pass. This has been my constant encouragement to my cousin Brittanie, to whom Sarah's letter is addressed.

We are introduced to Abraham and Sarah as Abram and Sarai at the beginning of their journey to Canaan. Abram was given the promise by God that he would be the father of many nations, and since Sarai couldn't bear any children, she felt that she needed to ensure the promise. Her decision was to give him Hagar, their handmaiden, to produce a son. When Hagar became pregnant and delivered Ishmael, she had contempt for Sarai and was out of order. She felt that this gave her a greater position over Sarai and treated her badly; then, Sarai asserted herself as the matriarch of the camp, and eventually Hagar ran away. An angel of God told her to go back and respect Sarai, because she was still a part of the covenant God had with Abram.

God told Abram that his people would endure four hundred years of enslavement. Then they would be delivered from the enemy and given the Promise Land. To seal the covenant of giving Abram's descendants favor, God asked Abram to look into the sky and count the number of stars. The stars were too numerous to count; so, too, would be the descendants of Abram. He then gave him a new name: Abraham, which means "father of many." To confirm that his wife was indeed a part of the covenant, he changed "Sarai" to "Sarah," which means "princess," as she would be the governess of Canaan, the land given to Abraham.

Years later, Sarah still had not given Abraham a son. By this time, Sarah was ninety, and Abraham was one hundred. Angels in the forms of herdsman come to Abraham's camp to tell him that he would bear a son with Sarah at the same time the next year. God is a faithful God; He always delivers just in time, His time. As the herdsmen stated, within the next year, she delivered their son and named him Isaac, meaning "laughter." This would be a constant reminder of how she had initially laughed at God's promise to her.

JUST-IN-TIME DELIVERY

Just-in-time (JIT) delivery is a term used in manufacturing that focuses on optimizing the delivery time of products to the customer. By ensuring that the focus is only specific to what, when, and how much is necessary, the delivery time for products to the customer are made right the first time and just in time.

Abraham went immediately the next day to follow God's Word and circumcised every male. Hagar and Ishmael laughed at Isaac, and Sarah was like, "They've got to go!" Abraham hated the decision he had to make, because Ishmael was his firstborn son. God told him he must send them on their ways because the promise had been given to the child that he and Sarah would have. It is interesting to note that the lineage of Ishmael would become the genesis of the Islamic religion, with Judaism and Christianity being of the lineage of Isaac. God truly blessed Abraham to be the father of many nations as he was the patriarch of the three monotheistic religions followed by over half of the world's population today.

There was one last test of Sarah's patience that she had to endure. Abraham followed God's Word and believed in all that He told him so that the promise would be fulfilled. He was requested by God to sacrifice his son Isaac. He had just lost his first son, Ishmael, and now he had to sacrifice the only son born to his wife. Once again, this had to be a difficult decision for him to make, but because of his diligence, He honored God's Word. As Sarah watched Abraham and Isaac go into the mountains, she knew deep down inside what Abraham intended to do. Since he didn't bring with him an animal sacrifice when they left, she knew Isaac would be the only option available. I can only imagine the hurt, pain, and distress she must have felt. She had waited ninety years for her blessing, her son, Isaac, just for him to be taken from her as he entered adulthood. Why would God give her a child in her old age, a child He ensured would be the son of His covenant? She didn't nag Abraham or speak to him directly about her concerns and worries. Instead of begging him not to take her only son, she trusted God. In trusting God, she knew that Abraham was following his responsibilities as expressly given to him by God. The ram in the bush was placed there by God just in time—nototot just on Abraham's behalf but on behalf of Sarah as well. They were in total order, allowing

God to be in total control. Because they both trusted God with their whole hearts, they were blessed as the mother and father of many nations.

RESILIENCE

We've all heard of the saying that patience is a virtue, a virtue that is very difficult for most of us to achieve. But it will take resilience in order to execute patience flawlessly. The definition of resilience is the power or ability to recover readily from adversity, from being bent, stretched, and returned to the original position. It's that hardheadedness, that "stick-to-it-ness," that "take a lickin' and keep on tickin'-ness" that keeps you going. And my loved ones have told me that I was always one hardheaded little girl. My resilience came from knowing that in the good times and the bad, all things would turn out to bless my life. God was in control, and if I was given a "no" in life, He would eventually turn it into a "yes."

Growing up poor and with adversity in New Orleans, I learned the ingenuity of how to make things work with what you've got. That turned me into the entrepreneur I am today. Back then, I learned how to make a dollar out of fifteen cents, and with these lessons, I teach other entrepreneurs how to make $1 million out of $15,000 today. What has been a constant thread throughout my life, my career, and my journey, is my belief in the power and providence of the Almighty Creator. Some would attempt to bend me too far to the left or to the right and try to convince me to doubt God's hand over my life. Whenever this occurred, my spiritual foundation is what anchored me back to center with my head due north. It kept me resilient and enabled my patience to endure.

As daughters of his covenant, our resiliency comes from a strong sense of purpose to pursue the legacies we will leave during our lifetimes. Even with all the cards stacked against us, we must be hardheaded enough not to panic. If we continue to trust in the Lord, He will reward our patience openly. Each second of resiliency will give us a daily portion of patience.

ENCOURAGEMENT EXERCISE: PRAYER

As the matriarch of the community, Sarah must have been a praying woman. She had to learn to pray, obey, and get out of the way. She had faith in God that He would bless her situation and do it in His own way.

Prayer is our special time to commune with God, to converse with Him for direction and understanding, and to gain comfort in what is happening in our lives around us. These conversations with God will mute our panic and build our patience in God's providence. (See the section entitled "Prayer: Our Conversations with God") Our patience will come from resilience, and our resilience will come from prayer.

There are four types of prayer that make up the ACTS model. ACTS stands for prayers of adoration, confession, thanksgiving, and supplication. Prayers of adoration are prayers that praise God's goodness, grace, and mercy. Prayers of confession are prayers that allow us to open up to God about our sins, repent, and ask Him for forgiveness. Prayers of thanksgiving allow us to thank God for His many blessings that He has bestowed upon us. And finally, prayers of supplication lift up requests to Him. We can go to God on our behalf or on the behalf of others. This prayer allows us to not only to bless our family and friends in our immediate circle but to also bless those around the world.

My encouragement to you is to make prayer not just a part of your daily routine, but make it instinctual. Our instinct should be to commune with Him as often as we can. Whenever we get inklings that it is time to speak with God, we must not hesitate; we must pray. Our prayers are always pleasant melodies to His ears and sweet aromas to His atmosphere. For all mothers who are having trouble with conceiving, I would like to leave you with a prayer of thanksgiving.

Dear Heavenly Father,
    We come before Your throne of mercy to ask that You anoint the wombs of those in need. Let them be open to receive God's seed. If You did it for Sarah in her old age, then You can do it again for our dear sisters. We thank God today that they are mothers

in the spiritual, and we speak a blessing of prophecy as we will celebrate You at this time next year as mothers in the natural. We thank You for Your anointing Spirit and that You will continue to give them the strength to endure. In the mighty, all-powerful, life-giving name of our Lord and Savior, we say amen!

Chapter 4

IN GOD WE TRUST

MIRIAM

BIBLE READING: EXODUS THROUGH NUMBERS
VIRTUE: TRUST

Dear Sister,

On that very day that my mom, Jochebed, put my baby brother Moses in the reed basket, I knew in my heart that God had a bigger plan for him. Our God of Abraham, Isaac, and Jacob had a promise for us to soon possess our promised land. But little did I know that my mom's action of trusting in God would be the start of that promise unfolding right before our eyes.

These were very hard times for us as Israelites. We were enslaved by the Egyptians and beaten daily. Even though we were able to worship God, we were constantly forced to believe in the many gods that they believed brought the rain, sun, and harvest. But as hard as these times were, our faith grew, and as our faith continued to grow, so did our numbers. Our population grew so large that it spooked Pharaoh into thinking we would stage a coup and overtake him and his people.

So, being the coward that he was, he exterminated all male Israelite babies. The wails and cries of the heartbroken mothers were just too hard to bear. But even in this despair, we still had great trust in the God of our ancestors. My mother knew my brother couldn't experience the same fate. And I knew that my baby brother Moses was special and that God had something for him. I was superprotective of him, just like any big sister would be. I watched him as he floated along the river to the other side. I said a prayer, let go, and let God! In my prayer, God answered, and His answer was one that let me still care for him from afar. He gave me the idea to offer my mom as the nursemaid for the new baby Pharaoh's daughter had found in the river. The "new" baby was my "old" baby brother. It was a perfect setup! This way, he could still be cared for by our mom; she could still love and protect him and keep him close.

With our mother's nurturing, he grew into such a strong leader. The combination of his Hebrew heritage and Egyptian upbringing created the best leader we could ask for to lead us to God's promise. His foundation was a strong faith in God and courage as a Hebrew. He supplemented this with the knowledge and power he obtained growing up as an Egyptian.

After he led us out of Egypt, I led the women in song and dance to praise the Lord for deliverance. "Ashira, Ashira, Yahweh, Yireh!" Along with my brother Aaron, I continued to be one of God's most trusted leaders as we traversed the wilderness for forty years. But even with all of the grace and mercy shown by God to me, I still doubted God. At the end of our journey, I doubted God's anointing in one key piece of the puzzle—the woman whom He had chosen for Moses's wife. It was my protection instinct kicking, which all big sisters fall prey to at one time or another. I pulled out my checklist. She was an Ethiopian; check! She wasn't one of us; check! She didn't believe like us; check! She didn't look like us; check! So I was sure that she wasn't a part of God's plan. Unfortunately, this one crack in my trust in God was my ultimate undoing. God condemned me with leprosy, and sadly I never got to see the Promise

Land. But, I rest in peace, knowing that my beautiful people finally reached their Promise Land flowing with milk and honey.

Shalom,
Miriam

TRUST

Miriam was the first prophetess identified in the Bible. A prophetess is defined as a woman who speaks for God or by divine inspiration. In order to speak for God, Miriam had to have a strong foundation of trust in Him—trust in God that what He decreed upon her was what she believed He would do for her and her people, God's people. We see in the story of Miriam that she walked in her anointing as a prophetess at an early age by ensuring that her mother became the nursemaid for Moses. She knew that God had something special in store for Moses. He would one day become the antithesis of Pharaoh and would reverse His power over the Israelites.

As Miriam witnessed the almighty power of God, her trust in God grew. He sent ten plagues as a punishment to Pharaoh for not obeying His orders to free the Israelites. Each of the ten plagues was directly connected to countering a specific god of Egypt. The turning of the Nile to blood was a direct threat to the Egyptian god Sobek. The plague of frogs was to intimidate those who worshipped Heket, the Egyptian god of fertility and renewal that had the head of a frog. It culminated with darkness, countering the power of the sun-god Ra. When Pharaoh would not acquiesce to God's demands, He ultimately countered Pharaoh's previous edict to decimate the population of the Israelites by killing firstborn Egyptian sons. The Egyptians believed that Pharaoh was a god in human form on earth and served him. But God had to prove that He was the only God to be served. God countered with the deaths of all firstborn sons not protected by His blood. He literally passed over the homes of Miriam and the others in the Israelite camp that had lambs' blood on their doorposts.

And this is why we celebrate Passover today. This confirmed for them that even as trials and tribulations may go on all around them, His anointing would still protect them.

Through her strong trust in God, Miriam experienced God's miracles of parting the Red Sea, delivering the Ten Commandments, and even protecting her brother. He not only survived the journey along the river as a baby, but he also thrived to become the very leader to usher in their promise. But interestingly enough, she didn't trust God's decision in His choosing of Zipporah as Moses's wife. Oftentimes we are just like Miriam because, in spite of all that God has done to show us that He is in control of all things and still on the throne, as soon as He does something that we may not agree with or understand, that bank of trust is no longer existent for us to withdraw from.

The story of Miriam and the Israelites also shows us how God will protect us in all stages of pursuing our destinies—before, during, and after reaching our promises. He builds our faith and trust in Him by not just the big, spectacular miracles like parting the Red Sea before the journey, but He also builds our trust in small, daily increments, like providing manna from heaven during the journey. Manna means "What is it?" in Hebrew. The Israelites didn't know what this white, flaky substance that tasted like honey was and why they couldn't gather and store it like other crops. What looked like coriander and tasted like wafers made with honey appeared overnight and covered the ground like dew or frost. It had to be gathered, baked, and eaten within the same day. God only made an exception of this daily spoilage for the Sabbath and allowed twice as much to be collected and stored in one day.

God made the manna expire daily to sharpen the faith of the Israelites. They had to believe that every day, God would deliver a new and fresh anointing that would sustain their lives for just another day.

And so it is with us in modern times. God continues this legacy to sharpen our faith in Him by giving us incremental blessings to get us to the next day, to the next stage. We must trust that the time, the energy, the finances, and the resources that God gives us for this day is enough. He will give us a fresh, new anointing daily.

OUT OF THE BLUE
This manna coming out of the blue sky was a shock to the Israelites. This is a possible origin of the phrase "out of the blue" to describe an event that is unexpected and without warning.

ARE WE THERE YET?

The story of the Israelites from Exodus through Numbers is my favorite of the Bible. It shows God's greatness and His faithfulness to bless us in spite of our complaining and disbelief. I feel very connected to the story of the Israelites—because, to be honest, I'm just like them because the closer I get to my destiny, the more and more trials come. In spite of all the miracles He unfolds before my eyes, I still huff and puff, murmur, and complain as the Israelites did. The only difference between my actions and that of the Israelites is that as my walk with Him in the wilderness progresses, my faith continues to grow, and my murmuring has now subsided only to thoughts.

My prayer is that as I continue my walk with Him, even my thoughts will disappear. This is my prayer for all of us, as we all are still works in progress just like the Israelites. Just like them, we have received our promises from Him, and just like them, we are still in a state of "Are we there yet?" More importantly, just like them, we know that all of our steps are ordered according to God's will. (Psalms 37:23).

The Israelites did not know the path and trusted in God as their GPS (what I like to call "God's Protective System") to illuminate their path and lead the way. Their steps were ordered by His Word, and He protected them from the Egyptians and other armies in the wilderness by His angels. Biblical scholars note that the Israelites took what would be considered the scenic route from Egypt to Canaan because they could have taken a more direct route to reach their destination. I can only imagine what many in the region probably thought: "What is up with those Israelites? And where are they going?" But no one could stop them from reaching their destiny. It is as if God protected them with a cloak of invisibility, and no one could touch His anointed.

Once they reached the Promise Land, all of their original leaders had perished—Moses, Aaron, and Miriam. They had all gone to be with their ancestors. As they continued to trust in God, He kept His hand of protection over His chosen people. He gave them a new leader in Moses's protégé, Joshua. Moses's combination of Hebrew heritage and Egyptian upbringing made him the perfect leader to reach the promise. In the same way, Joshua's combination of determination and warrior spirit made him the perfect leader to maintain the promise (Joshua 1:2–5).

<u>ENCOURAGEMENT EXERCISE: MANNA MOMENTS</u>

How many times has God been faithful in providing for us even when our faith in Him has been questionable? Seventy times seven comes to mind, which also is the number of times Jesus tells Peter he should forgive his brother when he sins against him (Matthew 18:22). Just as He forgives our sins of unfaithfulness, He wants us to forgive our brothers as well. The prayer Jesus gave us to honor God states, "Give us this day our daily bread" (Matthew 6:11). This is a reminder to us of how God provides us with a fresh, new anointing daily, just as he did with the Israelites in the wilderness.

Take a look back over your life, and find those moments when God has provided in spite of your unfaithfulness, those scary moments when you couldn't understand how God could put you through so much strife and pain and you couldn't see an end in sight. But then it seems as if out of nowhere, He provides. Things are not always what they seem, and God is working through all moments—the good, the bad, and the ugly. I like to call these moments "manna moments" when God provides us blessings incrementally, similar to the way He provided manna from heaven to the Israelites. Write these moments down in your passport journal with the date and how you felt during that time.

ON THE ROAD CALLED I-10: THE RISE

*On the road called I-10, is where it all began:
the balm for my wounded soul,
where I can be made whole
and start over once again.*

Interstate 10, or I-10, is one of the America's most-traveled highways, where I discovered my inner self and learned who I am. During my drive on I-10 along River Road lined with derricks, pipelines, and oil rigs, I was still a little girl. This is where my successful career in oil and gas started at just nineteen years old with not a care in the world.

Then in a second, in a minute, in an hour, it all changed. I found myself in my third semester of college, with child, and clearly with more questions than answers. I had just graduated from the largest high school in the state as number four in my class of 506. I was an all-star athlete, a college engineering student, a scholarship recipient, a Texaco INROADS scholar, and the list goes on. Just as my own universe started to take form, my world had begun to crumble. I thought, "I've disappointed everyone. What would they think of my dirty little secret?" I wondered, "How did I make this mistake?"

My "dirty" little secret became the fuel to light the fire inside me to persevere. Every morning, I would awaken early to take a summer engineering course. I sat among other future engineers with my focus slightly distracted as my motherly instincts of protection started to kick in. As the professor scribed quadratic and kinematic equations on the board, I thought, "I've really gotta get moving now because there is another human counting on me."

As I would leave class to drive to my internship, I put on my fire-retardant "Smurf suit," tying the top portion strategically around my waist to hide my pregnancy. I knew well enough to know that working at an oil-and-gas-production plant while pregnant was risky—not just with all the caustic chemicals that could cause prenatal issues but because of all the physical labor involved as well. I was climbing heat exchangers, twenty-thousand-gallon drums, water towers, and intricate piping. Every day I would continue this routine of hide-and-seek. I didn't want them to uncover what I was trying to hide. I didn't want anyone to seek the beautiful treasure inside of me.

You see, the world said I had only two choices to make, the two *a*'s: adoption and abortion. Do I take the path to the left and travel down the road of abortion? Or do I take the path to the right and choose adoption? But there was a third *a*; the road straight ahead was still the road less traveled. This is the road of acceptance. I knew in my heart that as a child of God, acceptance was the only choice—acceptance of the path God had created for me and the blessing He had bestowed upon me. In Mary's chapter, we will explore the virtue of acceptance and how this can be a key to living a purposeful life.

Chapter 5

ROXANNE, YOU DON'T HAVE TO PUT ON THE RED LIGHT

RAHAB

BIBLE READING: JOSHUA 2
VIRTUE: FAITH

Dear Blessed Woman of God,

    Fear and anxiety had overtaken my people. They were aware that the Israelites were rapidly approaching to take over the land promised to them by Almighty God. They'd heard of what this great God could do. They'd heard of the stories of how He punished the Egyptians and Pharaoh Ramses II for refusing to let His chosen people leave to pursue their chosen land. This land had been promised to them through the generations, as far back as Abraham, Isaac, and Jacob. Moses provided the law and led them out of Egypt and through the journey in the wilderness. Now, with Joshua at the helm, they were given power by God to fight and protect their new land.

My homeland of Canaan was a very special land, a strategic land bridge connecting Africa with Asia and Europe. It linked two great oceans (the Indian with the Atlantic), so it was very important in commerce, a valuable asset to the region that they were not willing to relinquish. Once the spies arrived in our fortress city of Jericho to scout out the area and report back to Joshua, word got back quickly to our king. He was determined to not let the Israelites encroach upon his territory. But there was no way that he could stop this; it was already ordained by God, the King of Kings. Thus, it would be so. Canaan was always the land of the Israelites and was just on loan to him by God for a short while.

The spies were looking for a place to hide from the search party sent by the king. I, being a believer, knew this was my chance to show I was indeed a child of God just like the Israelites. I trusted my gut and agreed to hide them in my roof. I felt deep down in my soul that God gave me a purpose that I just had to deliver.

Agreeing to support the Israelite spies was definitely an unpopular decision with my family. They thought this could set them up for persecution by the king for treason. They berated me with questions of how I could trust and believe these Israelite spies. For God's sake, I had just met these men. My response to them was that I was not trusting them because humans are flawed. But I was trusting in God and in the Word He gave to me. I trusted my gut and heeded His voice. It was almost as if He was speaking directly to me. He told me, "Rahab, you don't have to put on the red light. Those days are over; you don't have to sell your body tonight." You didn't think The Police came up with those lyrics all by yourself, did you? So I laid down my responsibility as a lady of the night for the ultimate responsibility of serving Him to expand His kingdom, protect His people, and bring them to the Promise Land.

I praised Him in advance, for I knew deliverance was near. His hand of protection would cover me and my family. The red rope wasn't their idea, but it was His idea, His reminder to me of His sovereignty and power. Red was the color of salvation for the Israelites in Egypt, and now red would become the signal of salvation for me and my family. I had a choice to continue to serve the pagan gods of Jericho, but I chose to serve Him. My faith was the key to my salvation. And for my obedience to Him, I was rewarded with being a matriarch of the bloodline of the Messiah, Jesus Christ. They called me a harlot, but He called me His own. My dear sisters, if you can only remember one *thing from my story, I wish for you to remember this it doesn't matter what you are called by others as long as you are called by Him.*

*Faithfully,
Rahab*

TRUST YOUR GUT

Sometimes you hear that voice that is unmatchable or get that feeling deep inside that's undeniable that assists you in making a critical decision. This is most commonly called your "gut" speaking to you. I like to think that GUT stands for God's unmistakable talk. It is not happenstance that your gut is located at the place where the womb resides. This is because when God gives you a vision, an idea, a purpose; it is as if you are pregnant with anticipation. You can feel it deep down inside that God has given you a purpose that you must deliver. But it must be all in God's time. Your delivery time is predicated on when God feels your purpose has been fully developed in mind, body, and soul. When it's time to push, you will feel this sense of expediency and excitement, a tickling deep within that signals when it is time to push and deliver your purpose to the world.

THE GUT
The gut can either be used to reference the midsection of the body or to define the courage and determination of an individual.

Oftentimes your GUT will be in direct contrast with traditional logic and all the puzzle pieces that are presented in front of you at the time. Trusting your GUT will often be the more unpopular decision to make, the one that others will frown upon. However, when you hear that voice of God, you must act. Act as if it's a matter of life or death, as your purpose is predicated on following God's voice and no one else's.

When Joshua sent the spies to Jericho to scout out the Promise Land, they entered into the house of Rahab, a prostitute. Upon arrival, they learned of the king's plot to find them and kill them. Rahab trusted her gut and devised a plan to hide and protect them under the thatch of her roof. She believed that Canaan was the land of the Israelites and took a leap of faith to execute a plan that could end in arrest or death for her. She must have heard the voice of God to guide her actions and to craft such a foolproof plan. Her only request of the spies was very selfless. She asked that they spare her and her family when they returned to overtake the land.

Their instructions to her were to place a red rope outside her window to indicate to the Israelite army to bypass her home. This is similar to how God instructed the Israelites to place the red blood of the first lamb to indicate their protection from the death angel. Through His power, God ensured that the death angel passed over those homes so that no one was killed. It is not ironic, nor is it happenstance, that Rahab was asked to use a rope of red. Red, the color of the blood of the sacrificial lamb, would signify God's presence of protection for her and her family. It is with this red rope that Rahab was given the most precious treasure that anyone can receive: hope. God not only fulfilled His promise to have the Israelite army pass over her home, but He exceeded it. Rahab, this woman of unknown origin, eventually became a great ancestor of Jesus, the Savior Who became the sacrificial lamb during the celebration of the great Passover (John 1:29). As He died on the cross, His red blood signified the washing away of the sins of humanity. His five *p*'s of faithfulness sealed the deal and signified His perfect plan: His presence, power, protection, provision, and fulfilled promises.

There are questions I ponder after reading the story of Rahab. Since Rahab was a part of the lineage of Jesus, was she the key to the deliverance of the Israelites after all? Did God purposefully have the Israelites wander for forty years in order to put Rahab in place? There are never definitive answers to God's plan. We just need to be at peace and know that God's plan is not for us to understand but for us to submit to and experience.

THE PERFECT PLAN

We meet Rahab in an exciting part of biblical history. The story of Rahab shows God's providence to His promise. The Israelites are ready to take possession of their Promise Land. The land flowing with milk and honey had been promised to them by God through Abraham (Deuteronomy 26:9). Now, many of those who were a part of the event that kicked off this promise coming to pass—the original Exodus from Egypt—were long gone. Those who were getting ready to enter the Promise Land were about two generations removed from witnessing the signs and wonders of the ten plagues and the miracle of manna and quail from heaven. Much of the appreciation for the God of Abraham, Isaac, and Jacob had waned, and much of the enthusiasm for honoring God had slowed. Their beloved Moses passed on to meet his ancestors, and Joshua was now appointed as the new leader of the tribe. He had the direction, and he knew the way to get them back on track.

God came to Joshua in a dream and told him that He would lead and guide him. God continued to speak to Joshua throughout his leadership very consistently, specifically, and faithfully. The consistency and faithfulness to carry out His plan is not in our time but His time. God operates and delivers blessings from generation to generation—in seasons, days, and years, just as God blessed earth on the fourth day of creation with light to manage time and provide a framework for how to measure existence, duration, and progress (Genesis 1:14).

Joshua and the other Israelites had experienced God's power daily as He provided manna and quail from heaven in the days they were in the wilderness. Over time, these days on their journey turned into forty years. In God's eyes, these years represented a season of protection, anointing, and grace in the wilderness. Moses led the Israelites through a season of slavery in Egypt to a season of exodus and wandering in the wilderness. With Joshua as their lead, they were ready for the season of possession and greatness in the Promise Land. The Israelites complained throughout the course of these seasons because they didn't see daily changes in their situation.

On the cusp of their season of possession, they reached an impasse at the Jordan River. This was eerily familiar to when they reached the Red Sea with the mighty Egyptian army behind them. What were they to do? How would they cross to reach dry land? Would the promise end in disappointment? But then something amazing happened. Joshua commanded them to step out onto the Jordan River, and the waters receded. God parted the Jordan River just as He parted the Red Sea. He repeated this action to express His five *p*'s of faithfulness to the Israelites. Joshua told the Israelites that this is proof that God would continue to fight their battles and drive out all the "-ite" enemies from their Promise Land; the Canaanites, Hittites, Hivites, Perizzites, Girgashites, Amorites, and Jebusites would all be defeated. To symbolize the fulfillment of the covenant, He ordered the Israelites to grab twelve stones, representing the twelve tribes of Israel.

Just as God asked Moses to raise his staff to part the Red Sea, He was very specific in His Word and His orders to Joshua. He asked him to find the twelve stones and place them strategically. It was in this instant that their season of wilderness turned into their season of promise. God continued to show the Israelites favor in this season of Joshua by knocking down the walls of Jericho and even causing the sun to stand still over Gibeon.

God will not just move mountains for those that believe, but He will even go as far as have the earth stand still so that His promise is fulfilled. But we can't expect to stay still, doing nothing, and expect God to bless us. The saying that actions speak louder than words also holds true for God. We can pray, beseech, and call on His name every minute of the hour. These are all good things. But it's not until we are obedient and step out on faith to complete the action required of us that He will bring forth His promises to us.

Oftentimes we can be just like the Israelites and complain away the days but miss how God progresses our lives through the seasons. God will always set things for our good and the promises He has given to us. We must remember that God's timing is not our timing, and He transforms a situation in an instant. However, it is imperative for us to go through certain seasons—some good and some not so good—so that His perfect plan can be put in order. Let His perfect timing keep you in perfect peace.

IN PURSUIT OF (IM)PERFECT PATTY

The Bible shows us time and time again how God used those deemed undesirable for His glory. Interestingly, these undesirables were all chosen by God to be matriarchs of Jesus Christ's bloodline. Rahab, Ruth, Bathsheba, and Tamar were all truly destiny's children. Rahab was a prostitute, a prostitute who began her life serving pagan gods (especially the moon god, as Jericho was the "moon city"). She was a woman of non-Jewish origin who was treacherous to her nation in siding with and hiding the enemy. Ruth was also a woman of non-Jewish origin. She was a widow from Moab, the nation originated from the incest of Lot and his daughters (Ruth 1–4). Bathsheba was an adulteress who slept with King David when her husband was away in battle. Not only did she sleep with a man who was not her husband, but she agreed to lie and participate in a plot to hide her pregnancy. If only she could get her husband to return from battle and lie with her, then no one would be the wiser about the origin of her pregnancy (2 Samuel 11). Tamar was a princess, raped and violated by someone that she trusted: her half-brother Amnon. Then to add insult to injury, he had her thrown out of the palace, as if she had been the one to commit the atrocious act. She was told to not speak about what happened and to hold her tongue since this would bring disgrace to the royal family (2 Samuel 13). Living a Godly life is not about living a perfect life. The Bible teaches us about how to live and deliver on God's promises for our lives through imperfection. He is in pursuit of Imperfect Patty to deliver on His perfect plan. He can see past the imperfection to deliver the impossible.

Once upon a time in my life, I became so neurotic in my pursuit of being Perfect Patty that I became too focused on myself and not on God. I was relentless in my pursuit of being the perfect sister, the perfect daughter, the perfect friend, and even the perfect wife. My focus on being perfect in the eyes of those around me was such an exhaustive task. Then when I grew tired of being Perfect Patty, I decided to overcorrect and try to be the very opposite with so much fervor that I overcorrected in my walk with God. My prayers of confession became exponentially higher than those of thanksgiving; I needed much forgiveness for the sins created as a result of my Frankenpatty monster.

But I thank God for His grace and mercy and His everlasting love and patience. He never leaves us, nor forsakes us, and He patiently waits for us to be obedient with His arms opened wide. God was waiting for me to finally realize that my destiny wasn't tied to my perfection in the eyes of others but to my imperfection in the eyes of Him.

Now, this was not meant for me to go and do what I wanted, when I wanted, and how I wanted. As my walk with God matured, I knew better, so I would be required of Him to do better. It was for me to know that all was forgiven and that my destiny was still before me. Just as with these matriarchs of Jesus, my new path was ahead, and my baggage can fly free with God.

ENCOURAGEMENT EXERCISE: JERICHO WALK

As the Israelites crossed the Jordan River, they thought that was it. They had finally reached the Promise Land and were ready to take possession and reap the benefits. But there was still one last barrier they had to overcome: the walls of Jericho. Jericho was a city with a fortress built around it for protection. Faced with a challenge that many would think as insurmountable, Joshua remembered the Word of God to him that every piece of land they would set their feet upon would be theirs. Joshua commanded the Israelites to march around the walls of Jericho for six days and on the seventh, to praise the Lord with a loud strong shout. Seven priests would blow seven trumpets made of rams' horns. The walls of Jericho were brought down, and God made it so that the walls fell outward, creating ramps that allowed the Israelites to run into the city and overtake it.

I was faced with obstacles in my life that I seemingly couldn't solve. As I solved one, another, greater enemy would appear in its place. I was in such despair as the enemy was overtaking every element of my life—my home, my children, and my husband. It was as if I could see the good life in front of me; my promise was before me, but there was a wall preventing me from access. So I turned to my Bible for an answer and came upon the story of the Israelites and the destruction of the walls of Jericho. All of the ingredients for blessings and favor were there; seven was the number of completion, an action in dedication to God and praise of Him in advance. I put the Jericho walk into action in my life, and immediately God put a hand of protection around my home and loved ones. The barriers to my promise were removed, and I continue to reap the blessings of Abraham to this day.

You may feel at times that the enemy has come into your home to defeat, kill, and destroy. Just when you think you are in a good zone and can breathe a sigh of relief, you are faced with another barrier to overcome. But healing can come from stepping out on faith and putting faith into action just as the Israelites did. My encouragement to you is to try this Jericho walk for yourself to overtake the enemy.

Start by gathering your Bible, inspirational music, and any blessed oils you wish to bring along your walk. Turn to Joshua 6, and read the scripture about the victory at the walls of Jericho as you walk around the outside perimeter of your home. As you continue your walk around six times, include prayers of thanksgiving to God for giving you victory in battle. You can also anoint the exterior of your home with blessed oils as you speak victory for all those who reside within it. If your neighbors have a look of confusion on their faces, tell them don't worry; victory is near. Then invite them to join you—the more the merrier. On the seventh time, begin to play your inspirational music. Heck, if you can find a trumpet, blow one! Give God a loud shout of praise, for the victory is won.

Chapter 6

GET IN FORMATION

DEBORAH

BIBLE READING: JUDGES 4
VIRTUE: LEADERSHIP

Dear Kayla,

When I served as the Queen Mother over Israel, many would come to meet me at my palm tree for advice and my best judgment on what to do next. I was the only female judge appointed to govern the Israelites—and the best, if I may say so myself—not because of my physical strength and power but because of the strength of my mind and heart. As you ladies say nowadays, "Girl power!" Many called me fearless, but my fearlessness didn't come from my own might but because I believed that with God on our side, we should fear nothing.

Now don't tell anyone I told you this; this is our little secret, but the Israelites were an absolute nightmare to deal with. All of the whining and complaining! "How do we defend ourselves against our enemies? Who will protect us? They are larger in number and have more chariots and armor than us; how do we compete?" It got on my absolute last nerve! Especially that nagging Barak. I couldn't believe their selective memory of totally forgetting about how God, through Moses, brought us out of bondage from Egypt, and then God through Joshua brought us into this wonderful Promise Land. So there shouldn't be any questions ever concerning these matters. If God did it before, then He will do it again.

They would inquire of me to solve their problems and to give them encouragement that God was still with them and that God still provides. And my answer to them was always this: "When you ask for God's help, He delivers—not half of the time, not some of the time, but all of the time. No problem is too hard for God to fix."

Now, I'm aware that you are dealing with some obstacles in school with chemistry and geometry. First, let me assure you that everything you need to overcome those obstacles is already inside of you. I will tell you the same thing that I told Barak so that he could triumph over the one-hundred-thousand-strong army of Sisera: you have all of the brainpower and intelligence already inside of you; you just have to tap into this through the help of God. Just as God appointed Joshua and Moses to help my people, He appointed those adults around you to support and nurture your success in life. Your parents, teachers, and your family are all given to you as gifts from God to protect, serve, and pull the best out of you. I want you to do as I did and find your "palm tree"—your place of serenity. Take your problems to God in prayer, and watch Him provide all that your heart desires. Always remember that there is no obstacle too big for God to help you overcome, and there is no problem too big that you cannot solve.

Sincerely,
Deborah, the Queen Bee

GOD'S PROTECTION PERSONIFIED

It's interesting that we don't hear many sermons using the book of Judges. I feel there are many valuable lessons that we can glean that are relevant to the social and political climate of today. Deborah's letter is addressed to my teenage daughter Kayla. I believed that Deborah's voice could assist me with guiding my daughter into defining her own path as a self-sufficient young woman and leader. Judges talks of the craziness with God's people after He did all of that work with getting them out of the hands of Pharaoh, out of the hands of Egypt, out of the house of bondage. After spending forty years in the wilderness, they were finally in the Promise Land. And then now, they start to act a fool. Moses's mission for God's people was finished, and he appointed his mentee, Joshua. But they gave poor Joshua such a hard time that he said it's better off to be up there with the Lord than to try to wrangle you fools down here in Canaan (Joshua 24:14–29).

Canaan was an important city at the crossroads of three major empires, so people had to deal with a lot of strife and fighting with the Egyptians, Hittites, and Assyrians. God even tried to use this as a wake-up call to get them to act right but to no avail. Now God was left with a conundrum in how to govern His people so that they will act right versus letting them just run amok and destroy His land, the land He had promised to His people. They had no one to keep them on the straight and narrow path and not follow the religions of the Canaanites. And so He came up with the idea to appoint leaders—or judges, as they were called—to provide deliverance to His people. The judges were sent to govern as leaders and put them back on the path of right. They personified God's presence, power, protection, provision, and fulfilled promises.

Every time the Israelites repented of their sins, God would send another ruler or judge to lead them, and He would forgive them. This cycle lasted through twelve judges. The judges were not appointed by heredity, as would be the case in a monarchy, but all were divinely appointed for such a time as this (Esther 4:14). This shows how God will call individuals to be leaders, those who willingly offer themselves to His service regardless of their background or lineage.

Here enters Deborah, the fourth judge and only woman appointed to rule over God's chosen. Deborah's purpose was to ensure that the

Israelites honored the commandments and that they remained protected from the Canaanites. Judges 4 begins with a revolutionized military strategy for the Canaanites who still occupied Canaan because iron was now used in the creation of weaponry, chariots, and armor. There were growing concerns among the Israelites, and they had just as many questions as they did soldiers at that point. But Deborah had the answers; she had the strategy, and she chose Barak as the military leader to execute her strategy.

The answer from God was to send a rainstorm to overtake and drown the mighty chariot army. Her strategy from God was to send the ten thousand soldiers to attack after the flooded and muddy Kishon River had overpowered the Canaanite army. Her leader, Barak, was called by God to lead the charge until victory was won. Girl power was in full effect as the Canaanite general Sisera was also slain by a woman, Jael.

In her role, she was seen as the mother of Israel, the queen called to govern. Her name, "Deborah," means "bee" in Hebrew, so this makes her the original Queen Bee. (Yes, you read that right; there was someone crowned the Queen Bee way before Beyoncé was appointed to this throne by her Beehive.) And just like Beyoncé, she empowered the masses through the words of her song, even telling her people to *get in formation* some thousands of years ago. In Judges 4:6, we find her encouraging the Israelites, saying, "Come on, y'all. Let's get in formation, Israelites! It's time for you to prove to me that you've got some coordination." She tells Barak, "It's time to slay; it's time to fight!" In chapter 5 after the victory and triumph over the Canaanites, she pens a song with Barak and shows that she is quite the songstress herself.

Those who knew Deborah, knew that they could find her by a palm tree. This tree is symbolic because palm trees were very rare in Palestine at that time. Thus, she could say, "You can find me by the palm tree," and everyone knew where she was. It was her place of calm, a place of reflection where she could clearly hear from God. Palm trees stand for peace and plenty. In the New Testament, when palms were lain at Jesus's feet, they led to the path of victory and led to the triumphant arrival of Jesus (John 12: 12–15). They represent victory of the spirit over flesh.

Despite all of the foolishness and cantankerous chicanery that was going on in Israel at that time, she was able to find her place of refuge. She would go to her palm tree and get a Word from God for His people. We should all take a page from Deborah's book and find our own places of respite, places to hunker down despite all of the foolishness from our family, all of the foolishness from our friends, and all of the foolishness going on in the world. It is a requirement: we must, as the Queen Bees of our hives, find our resting places, our home bases where we can clearly serve our purposes and hear the Word of God. And when we get this Word, we should deliver it to His people, starting with "Thus said the Lord!" This is because people need to not see us; they need to see that we are speaking the Word that our Lord and Savior has placed in our hearts. When we speak a Word over them, it's not about us, but it's about God and the Word He has given us.

SO WHAT IF MY CHROMOSOMES MATCH?

Every morning I awaken, just like the 3.7 billion of women around the world, to go into the battlefield and fight to be accepted, utilized, valued, and celebrated in male-dominated environments. We slap on our war paint (a.k.a. makeup); war gear (a.k.a. skirts and SPANX—oh my!); and our war shoes (a.k.a. our heels that enter us into another silent battle we didn't even sign up for by wreaking havoc on our feet more than anything else). Just as we are meticulous about putting on our war gear, we need to be even more diligent in putting on the whole armor of God (Ephesians 6:11–18).

Ephesians 6:12 states that we are wrestling against principalities, the rulers of darkness, and spiritual hosts of wickedness. By girding our waists with truth, putting on the breastplates of righteousness, the gospel of peace, and the helmets of salvation, we will be victorious over the wiles of the evil one. And when we head out of the door, let's not forget to pick up our power bags. These will carry our shields of faith and the swords of the Spirit as you get ready to enter the battlefield.

I used to become exceedingly frustrated with having to prove myself over and over again simply because both of my chromosomes matched. I grew tired of metaphorically having to "throw my résumé" on the table in every team meeting or presentation or to prove myself, even during the times where I was front and center as the instructor. I always possessed the skills, capabilities, and talents to be effective. Why was this always so difficult?

Or ladies, how about the times in which you provide a credible solution to a problem, and you are so confident in your response, knowing that this was the perfect answer? In your mind, you envision yourself dancing, doing the tootsie roll and cabbage patch in the end zone and spiking the ball while saying, "Touchdown, baby! I know everyone is gonna like my idea!" Then, you are brought back to the reality that no one seems to have heard you, and to add insult to injury, someone of the XY persuasion speaks up and says the exact same thing you've just said. He is applauded and lauded for his fantabulous contribution. Then, that vision in your head quickly turns from an end-zone celebration to you turning red and tackling everyone on the sidelines.

The movie *Hidden Figures* explores how a group of women successfully navigated the male-dominated environment of NASA in order to be valued for their intelligence. They were key components to the progression of the program in mathematics and scientific computations, which ultimately led to putting a man on the moon. These monumental advancements in human life didn't just make a splash here locally in the United States but also had an international impact. Since the United States was the first to land a man on the moon, we were able to win the space race with the Soviet Union for world supremacy.

Recently, I had the pleasure of meeting the granddaughter of Katherine Johnson, the great NASA mathematician chronicled in *Hidden Figures*. Katherine Michele Sanders and I were selected by Louisiana State University to provide our thoughts on this inspirational movie and to speak about how we can increase the representation of women in the science, technology, engineering, and math (STEM) fields. It was an honor to sit alongside her and other great women and to provide advice to empower the next generation of female STEM leaders.

What I learned from her granddaughter is that these courageous women were simply pursuing their God-given destinies. They answered God's call to leadership and indirectly were able to make a global impact on politics. They faced many obstacles along their paths in having to overcome what I call the "label trifecta." They were undervalued and underutilized simply because they were young, black, and women. Just like these trailblazers, I've personally learned early on in my adulthood to not use my trifecta as a shield and create a barrier to those who may discredit my abilities because of these neutral labels but to turn this shield on its head into a silver platter used to deliver the best value to those same people who would discredit me.

TO THE MOON AND BACK
An organization created by the granddaughter of Katherine Johnson that encourages young women to pursue STEM education. This is in honor of her grandmother, who continues to tell her to this day that she loves her "to the moon and back."

Because of their mere existence in their God-given bodies, they were undervalued and underutilized. Most importantly, because of their sheer persistence and faith in God, they consistently stayed on their paths to purpose. They were fierce before being fierce became popular. Their fierceness came from not just understanding Ephesians 6 but from internalizing this scripture. They knew that their fight was not against the men who told them that they couldn't, shouldn't, and wouldn't amount to anything. They knew their fight was against the powers of the evil one and that this was simply a trick of distraction employed to derail them from their destinies. Armed for battle, they redirected their energy from repaying the evil with evil and placed it into singlehandedly advancing humankind. Day in and day out, these "hidden figures" embraced the fact that whenever they first entered into a room, they would have to overcome the label trifecta. By donning their war gear in the natural and the whole armor of God in the spirit, they were more than conquerors.

There are many women throughout history who were called to lead armies of men, many of whom doubted their leadership. In the 1500s, Queen Elizabeth was lauded for bravely leading the charge into battle wearing her tailor-made suit of armor. In the 1100s BC, Queen Bee Deborah led the Israelite army valiantly equipped with her tailor-made spiritual suit of armor protecting her mind, body, and spirit. At times, it may be difficult for us as women to be respected as leaders in male-dominated environments. But we make the best leaders because we have the abilities to lead with our heads and with our hearts. Let's take a page out of Deborah's book and float like a butterfly, but sting like a bee. Let's lead boldly together!

ENCOURAGEMENT EXERCISE: PALM PLACE

You are the Queen Bee over your hive. The purpose God has over your life is to midwife the destinies of those around you into the world. From the outside looking in, a beehive looks like a mess, with bees going in a ton of different directions. But on the inside, there is a method to this madness because the queen is in total control. The queen bee's responsibility is to stay put in one location and deliver on her purpose to make honey for the hive. She knows that this is where she must stay, where she must call home base, because she's got work to do! Just like hives, from the outside looking in, our lives can look like messes, with all the craziness and people going in different directions. It is critical that we find our central locations, take control, and lead.

My encouragement to you is to find your place of respite in your home. Find a small nook, a corner, a designated area where you will be able to find peace. This is your place where you can pray, meditate, and honor your relationship with God. This place of serenity will help you to hear God's voice clearly and give you clarity in direction for yourself and for those around you. In your "palm place," you can place items that bring you peace and also those that encourage your creativity. In the movie *War Room*, we saw the protagonist of the movie remove the items from her personal closet and turn this into her palm place. This was her war room where she prayed for the repair of her marriage and was ultimately successful in keeping her family together as a single unit.

My palm place is a small closet under my stairway—a Harry Potter closet, if you will—where I retreat to pray, meditate, and hear from God. This is the place where my creativity flows the most freely, and where I feel the closest to my purpose. I have anointing oils and special items such as a crystal butterfly that represents my grandmother's continual presence in my life. I have a pen and paper close by to capture the thoughts and ideas given to me by God in my special place. I also have a prayer board on which my husband and daughters can place their prayer requests on Post-its so that when I go to God in prayer, I can go on their behalf. Sometimes our love ones have a hard time telling us their wants and needs out of shyness and have fears of saying them out loud. This helps with encouraging them to communicate things they are asking for and need direction on. Just like Deborah, they know that when I'm at my palm place, I'm going to God on their behalf. They are ready for me to deliver the words of advice that I have for them that are in alignment with God's divine order.

Chapter 7

WIDOW'S PEAK

RUTH

BIBLE READING: RUTH 1-4
VIRTUE: LOYALTY

Dear Sister,

"Our God is an awesome God. He reigns from heaven above. With wisdom, power, and love, our God is an awesome God." I would sing this beautiful melody every day as I picked the sheaves of grain. It had been quite some time since the passing of my husband, but instead of sadness, my heart was filled with encouragement—encouragement that my God of wisdom, power, and love would take care of me in my time of need. I was eternally grateful to my husband for introducing me to a love that surpasses all and endures all: the love of God.

As a Moabitess, I grew up serving idols like Chemosh, Baal, and others. There wasn't a connection with any of these deities; it was just a one-way street of loyalty born out of legacy and not love. This one-way street often left me feeling empty and searching for more. Then I met my husband, and I found what I was searching for. He showed me true loyalty. He showed me the God of Abraham, Isaac, and Jacob. He showed me the God Who loved His Chosen people, the people He chose to provide for in all of their needs—even the basic need of providing daily sustenance, which He provided by raining manna down from heaven. Yes, you may think that as his wife, I had no choice but to serve his God. But I didn't serve his God out of obligation; I chose God out of love. I was excited to know that because I chose Him, I was now one of His chosen, and He would provide for and protect me still the same.

Besides, this was the same God Who saved my great ancestor Lot from perishing as Sodom and Gomorrah were destroyed. God's love provided for my dearest Mahlon and sustained him during the famine. When I accepted his hand in marriage, I was ridiculed by my fellow Moabites. They would tell me, "Those Israelites are just full of stories of their God. Where is their God now? Why would He bring a famine to His chosen ones?" My answer to them was that God is an awesome God. He knows all with His wisdom, He controls all with His power, and He provides to all with His love. This was soon made abundantly clear through my journey from wife to widow and back again. Because I became a widow, I experienced the peak of my life.

After the deaths of all the men in our family, the Moabite community thought of Naomi as a black widow. They thought that everything she touched perished and even joked that she probably was the reason for the famine in Jerusalem. They would say that she touched the crops, and they died. How awful! They begged me to stay away from her because I could be next. But she told Orpah and me that she wanted to return to her homeland to live out her last days in more comfort. She insisted we stay with our family because we were young and could find husbands and start over again.

My loyalty to God drew me closer to Naomi, and I knew my purpose was in front of me. My purpose was to continue to care for my mother-in-law. Not only is this what my darling

Mahlon would have wanted, but most of all, this is what God wanted. By showing loyalty to Naomi, I was able to show my undying love for God.

Sincerely,
Ruth

THE RECIPE FOR SUCCESS: PERSEVERANCE, PRAYER, AND PEOPLE

This story is often told as one to encourage a woman that her "Boaz" is out there and that he will find her. The focus is mainly on how Naomi prepared Ruth and told her "Go get your man!" But a critical element that is always absent in the recanting of this story is that Ruth was serving in her God-given purpose. Her main focus was not to search for a new husband but walking in her purpose, which was to care for her mother-in-law. The story should serve as encouragement to women, especially widows, that they can still reach the peaks of their lives after experiencing their pits.

Ruth was from Moab, and Moabites were not a celebrated people. The Israelites considered the Moabites distant relatives but didn't always get along with them. They were shunned because the Moabites are descendants of Lot from an inexcusable act. One night, his daughters got him drunk and had sex with him in order to procreate, creating the people of Moab. Thus, Ruth deciding to stay loyal to her mother-in-law, and returning to Bethlehem was a unique and probably very unpopular opinion among her Moabite family.

There was a drought in Bethlehem, and a husband and his wife, Naomi, took their two sons east into Moab. Then, while in Moab to find sustenance, their sons took Moabite women to marry. Then, all three men died, and the widow women were left alone to fend for themselves. It was at this time that Naomi told both her daughters-in-law to go back to their mothers and to the comfort of their homes. After much consternation, Orpah agreed to go. Naomi thought for sure that Ruth would return to her family as her sister Orpah did. Naomi actually encouraged it. Ruth insisted on walking in her purpose by staying loyal to Naomi.

As it was with Naomi, she was okay with letting Orpah return to her family because it was the time for her to go. Her season in her life had come to an end. She was comfortable in knowing that Ruth's acceptance to continue with her was ordained by God. Ruth would be the resource to enable her to continue her life's journey. With Ruth by her side as her kindred spirit, she would be once again connected to her kindred. This created an even more unbreakable bond between her and Ruth. They had been there for each other as they mourned the deaths of their husbands, but Ruth now chose the more difficult route, and for this, Naomi was eternally grateful. The journey back to her homeland was a part of God's plan, as He had a plan to supply all of their needs through this kindred-spirit connection.

When they arrived at the Bethlehem grain fields, they learned that the Israelite harvesters were only allowed one pass through the fields, and then the poor were able to pick up the leftovers. As widows, Naomi and Ruth were considered poor and at the bottom of the list for harvesting as well as for the receiving of inherited land. Because Naomi was old in age, Ruth would go out by herself daily to gather these leftovers. And this is when Boaz saw her, while she was walking in her purpose to care for Naomi. He was immediately enamored with her outer beauty. But most of all, he was drawn to her because she was walking in her purpose by caring for Naomi. She showed loyalty by sticking it out with her through the rough times.

He was so in awe of her loyalty that he instructed a group of women harvesters to leave a little extra for her to collect in order to prepare meals for her and Naomi. To show his dedication to her, he also provided for her safety and sustenance by allowing her to eat with his workers and drink from his well. He inquired of her and determined that he could indeed take her as his bride. She was the widow of his distant cousin Mahlon, and it was customary for the relative of a deceased man to marry his widow and ensure that she was cared for.

Naomi reciprocated her loyalty by preparing Ruth to take Boaz as her husband according to Israelite custom. She directed Ruth to put on her finest robes and sweetest perfume to slip under and cover his feet. Then, according to custom, Boaz sealed the covenant by placing his shawl over her head in a promise to cover her for the rest of her life. Ruth was a new convert to the God of the Israelites. Yet, through her loyalty to God, she showed His love more than those who were born into it. Ruth's loyalty to God equated to compassion for her mother-in-law. Her love and care of Naomi provided her with a happily ever after: a husband, land, and a part of the lineage of the Lord and Savior, Jesus Christ.

Faith in God is what kept Ruth grounded through the roller coaster of life. When she truly believed that the Higher Power was in control, she had a sense of freedom and peace. She had the freedom to persevere what occurred in her, the good and the bad, because she knew it was a part of His larger plan. Through continual prayer, she remained accountable to her vertical relationship with God. Remaining accountable to her vertical relationship with God provided the fertilizer to grow her horizontal relationships with the people around her.

The lesson we can take from Ruth is that when we have a greater sense of loyalty, then we will have a higher level of integrity. Our code of ethics in how we engage with others will grow. In the most famous code of ethics of all time, the Ten Commandments (Exodus 20:1–17), six of the Ten Commandments provide guidance on how we treat each other. This proves to me that God places a significant importance on how we interact with other humans who inhabit this earth with us. You can't say that you love the Lord without showing God's love to the people around you.

LOYALTY, LOYALTY, LOYALTY

While serving in a community-based organization, I witnessed the systematic dismantling of the house that loyalty built. I was left thinking. As women navigating our male-dominated day, we have ninety-nine problems to endure; why make the disloyalty of each other one of them? The clever use of rewritten laws and unwritten rules was eerily familiar to what had kept us as women relegated to domestic duties with no clear decision-making power in the past. We were only provided with the right to vote in 1920; it kept us from having choices in the realm in which we lived. Even as überproud as I am as a Black American, I still find it appalling that we as women were not provided the right to vote until 1920. This was some fifty years after Black American men were given the right to vote.

In this organization, there was an equal split of power among women and men. But even after we reached equality in the voting process, the decision was made to not elevate one of our own—one of our own with a proven track record of loyalty to the organization with the gifts of her time, money, and intellect in hopes of catapulting this organization to the pinnacle of the community. Her loyalty, her faithfulness, and her commitment to the advancement of women in this organization was to be applauded and rewarded in kind. Unfortunately, when provided the opportunity to show their loyalty to God by treating their fellow sister with love, care, and respect, they did not reciprocate. To add insult to injury, this organization hosted a women's empowerment day for the community, a big love fest for women to encourage each other on a macro scale. Ironically, they missed the opportunity to display this same love to one of their own in their immediate circle on a micro level.

My counsel to this sister through her tears was to focus on the three *p*'s to continue her success in the community. Through her faith in God, she would persevere through this lapse in judgment by those in her circle. Go to Him in prayer for direction and guidance of your next steps. Her destiny was still ahead of her, and this was merely a stop on the road in order to let some people off. Last, but certainly not least, she has to not lower, not raise, but adjust and optimize her expectations of the people around her.

As God continues to enlarge our territory, He will reduce our circle. Not everyone that was there at the beginning of your journey will be there in the apex. Most people will not share in the happiness of your success. It is frustrating because logically you would think that since people were there in the beginning for the struggles in the valley, they would equally support you in your peaks. But don't fret; God's got your back!

There are two types of people in your life: the vital few and the trivial many. Those who continue to reciprocate loyalty to you throughout your life are the vital few. Keep them close as they will make themselves known throughout your life by reciprocating loyalty. The trivial many are only on your train headed toward destiny for a period of time. When you know you have arrived at their stops, be sure to let them off. If you let people continue in your life past their seasons and their reasons, they will eventually commit treason against you. With God as your main source, He will continue to provide you the resources you will need to continue along your journey.

THE PARETO PRINCIPLE
Vilfredo Pareto was an Italian economist who determined that 80 percent of the wealth in Italy was held by 20 percent of the people—ttthe vital few. He called the rest of the population "the trivial many." This principle is com-monly called the 80/20 rule today.

ENCOURAGEMENT EXERCISE: FRIEND-VENTORY

There comes a time in every woman's life in which she must do the inevitable: take inventory of each individual in her life and determine whether he or she has the proper fit, form, and function for her life.

Most companies schedule inventory assessments or "take inventory" on a monthly basis. This is critical because as shipments of new products arrive, they have to make room on their shelves for placement. As a little girl, I can vividly remember my aunt Beatrice completing this exercise at the pharmacy store she managed. She would take a list of all the items that were available and determine if the item met the criteria for fit, form, and function. She would ask herself the following: Does the item fit within the sales goals we are trying to achieve? Does it have the right form that appeals to our customers? Does it have the optimal functionality that our customers desire? The items that didn't meet the criteria were identified as obsolete and first reduced to be sold at a discount rate. If this was not successful, they were recycled. And if no one wanted the items, then they were finally replaced.

Companies like Apple use an approach called "planned obsolescence," in which they force their products to become obsolete and plan this into the design. They plan for the obsolescence of their products so that they can constantly introduce something brighter, bolder, and better for the consumer. I believe that God does the same for the people in our lives to ensure that we have the right people in the right place at the right time to reach our destinies. He plans for the obsolescence of certain people in our lives as well. Then when we least expect it, someone enters our life who is bolder, brighter, and more amazing. God gives us some friends for a season and some friends for a lifetime.

With the friend-ventory exercise, we will determine their fit, form, and function for your life. To begin the friend-ventory exercise, brainstorm and capture on a sheet of paper all of the friends in your life. Then on a separate sheet of paper, create three columns. The headers for these three columns will be Name, Past Loyalty, and Present Loyalty. Write the names of your friends in the first column. For each friend, ask yourself two questions: (1) whether you can remember a time when this friend has shown you loyalty in the past; and (2) whether you can remember this friend showing you loyalty recently. Place a Y for yes and an N for no to answer these questions.

Now take a look at your list. Those friends with two Y's are your "ride-or-die" chicks and will be there for you through thick and thin. For those with at least one N, assess the roles they should play in your life; will it be a starring role or one of a recurring character? Will they support you in making it to the next level in your life?

For those with two *N*'s, forgive the person for any past hurts the person may have caused you (real or imaginary). Show compassion to these people because it is very likely that they were dealing with pain of their own that has caused them to hurt you. Repent to God, and ask for forgiveness for any malicious thoughts, words, deeds, or ill will you may have shown toward them. Wash, rinse, and repeat!

Chapter 8

HIDDEN IN PLAIN SIGHT

ESTHER

BIBLE READING: ESTHER 1–10
VIRTUE: COURAGE

Dear Fellow Queen,

I address you as "queen" because God has endowed us all as queens in our own right. When you have been called to a position of authority, you have to be brave and be ready to fight for what you believe in. As God grants you favor in His sight, He is telling you that you have been anointed and appointed for such as time as this. It's not about the position, but it's about the purpose. The position is simply the conduit to accomplish the assignment that God has placed on your life. I encourage you to stand up for what you feel is right.

This is why I honor Queen Vashti, who came before me as my "shero." King Ahasuerus had requested her presence after much celebrating with his friends. She was well aware of their bachelor-party, Hangoveresque antics, and she felt very uneasy in going before him in this situation. Full of wine, they were not in their right minds. Who knew what they might be capable of? Within her conscience, she was torn. Should she choose her truth or choose tradition? In this moment she thought about all the women who looked up to her as queen. She took a stand before them and refused to go before the king. Little did she know that her taking a stand when she was given the opportunity set the stage. The fact that she did not hesitate to do so helped me to know exactly what to do when my time came.

I'm pretty sure in reading my story of ascension to the throne that many of you felt a bit of beauty-pageant vibes. I'm also aware that in your society today, there are mixed feelings about the purpose of pageants, and mixed messages are portrayed about the role of femininity in society. It begs the question: How does this sort of forced ranking of women based upon their outer appearances affect the advancement of female equality? How can we shout from the mountaintops that we wish to be respected for our intellect and our values if we still support the placement of one woman over another based solely on her appearance?

But what you must understand is that this was the norm in my culture at this time. I had to trust the process because it would lead to my purpose. I was brought in by my cousin Mordecai to put my hat in the ring, if you will. It was quite the ordeal. According to protocol, I was assigned a team of seven who prepared me with oils and rituals for months. I was primped, plucked, and tucked in just the right way so that I could receive the favor of the king. Like I said before, sounds a lot like a beauty pageant, huh? Ha!

What they didn't know is that I already had the favor of the Almighty King, and His protocol had already been established. For He had already adjusted the eyes of King Ahasuerus so that I would find favor in his sight. When it was finally time for me to go before him, it was already a done deal. It wasn't about if I could be queen or if I should be queen—I would be queen. God's placement of me in a position of authority was not for my personal gratification; it was so I could be a blessing to my people and save His chosen people from being exterminated.

I believe that life is the finite amount of time bestowed upon you by the Creator to manage and manifest the energy that the Creator has gifted to you. Energy is never created or destroyed but is passed from one life force to another. Dr. Maya Angelou said it best when she described your duty: "If you get, give, and if you learn, teach." If I may be so bold,

I would add this "If you are favored, bless" during your lifetime, this finite amount of time you're given on this earth.

Sincerely,
Queen Esther

WHO DO YOU THINK YOU ARE?

Esther embodies the message of this inspirational quote by Oprah Winfrey: "I still have my feet on the ground; I just wear better shoes." Esther was handpicked at just the right moment to be queen. God hid her in plain sight and prepared her to be the advocate for her people at just the right time. At this time in history, men saw women only as serving the following purposes: sustenance, procreation, and pleasure at their behest. Especially as a queen at this time, you were only able to see your husband when he requested for you. And when he requested, you had to hasten to his request, and you were never to refuse it, no matter the time or day or reason.

When I was first introduced to the story of Esther some time ago, I initially thought it was a tale of two ladies in disparity. I thought the focus was on the contrast between the actions of Vashti and Esther and to show how one's actions were more respectful than the other. Besides, what else was I supposed to surmise as I was presented in sermons time and time again with a dichotomy of character traits—Vashti as defiant and Esther as humble? It wasn't until I reread the book of Esther that I truly understood that there were more similarities in the actions of these women than differences. In fact, Vashti was a trailblazer for Esther and set the stage for the ultimate redemption of her people.

King Ahasuerus had enjoyed the company of his companions with much food and much drink for a long period of time. Needless to say, they were pretty drunk when he requested her presence to show off to the group and prove that he had the most beautiful queen of them all. Queen Vashti felt very uncomfortable about going to the king under these conditions. She had never defied his order before as her husband and as her king, and this was foreign territory for her. She was faced with a pretty difficult decision to make. Does she follow tradition and follow his orders? Or does she follow her truth and face the possibility of harsh consequences? She then thought of all of the women both inside her kingdom and out and how she could take a stand for all of them who looked up to her as queen. She was courageous enough to take the more unpopular decision and refused to stand before the king. By not standing before the king, she took a stand for what was right. And Esther surely took note.

This decision sent shock waves throughout the community. From as far east as India to as far west as Libya, men were in fear that this would influence their wives to defy their husbands. But on the other side of the argument, the women were not seeing Queen Vashti's stance as an act of defiance but as an act of courage. She'd always shown absolute respect to the king. She just wanted him to respect her just the same. She wanted him to show respect to her by honoring her wishes. The chatter probably lasted for not just days, weeks, or months but for years and years. The men just would not let this go. I'm sure there were shouts to Queen Vashti: "Who do you think you are? How dare you? You must be dethroned!"

The men implored of him that this was not a simple act of defiance but an act of treason—one that could have ripple effects in the kingdom for years and years to come. Of course, the outrage by the men pushed King Ahasuerus to not only banish Queen Vashti from her throne but execute an edict to force women to follow every single order from their husbands, even if the orders put them in potential harm or danger. He then issued a call across the Persian Empire to find the next queen.

Enter Esther, a Jewish girl raised by her cousin Mordecai. Her father and mother had passed, and Mordecai took her under his wing and raised her. He protected her by changing her Jewish given name of Hadassah to a Persian one of Esther. The favor of God was bestowed upon Esther since birth, and she would undoubtedly be favored by everyone to whom she was introduced. Mordecai served as a member of the king's court and as one of his most trusted advisors. As a Jew, Mordecai refused to bow before Haman, the king's highest-ranking official. This is something that offended him greatly. He was determined to not only repay Mordecai for not bowing to him but to find a way to exterminate all of his people, the Jews, who he felt were becoming a nuisance across the land. King Ahasuerus asked all of his officials, including Haman and Mordecai, to bring him suitable candidates for marriage.

The candidates participated in a year of preparation with the finest oils, creams, and perfumes from across the empire. Esther was favored over the women by the chief eunuch and was given a double portion. With the official preparation period complete, it was finally time for the women to meet the king. As favor was her middle name, it was no surprise that the king selected her. As soon as he laid eyes on Esther, his heart was filled with joy. The king had spoken; a Jew would be Persia's next queen.

During her reign, Queen Esther was made known of Haman's plot to exterminate the Jews by her cousin Mordecai. Haman had the king to unknowingly sign a decree that would rid a race of people who posed a threat to his kingdom and refused to obey his laws. Once the king signed a decree, it was required to be executed just as stated. This grieved Esther's heart greatly. She knew with her position as queen that she had to do something. But she had to be careful in determining a plan to best help her people, for her being a Jew was still a secret, and the king was not aware that he had decreed his most favored to death.

She went to God for direction and asked her fellow Jews to fast for three days as His plan was revealed unto her. Her plan was smart but simple: play to Haman's ego and pride by inviting him to dinner with the king. He would excitingly take the invitation to be honored before the king. Then she would reveal to him that Haman's plot to exterminate her people behind his back. There was only one problem; she had not been asked by the king to come before his presence in thirty days. How would she be able to set her plan in motion?

Esther remembered the shouts of those who had opposed Queen Vashti's decision and gazed at herself in the mirror to say "Who do you think you are?" This time those words gave her the confidence she needed to remind herself that she was not only a woman but a brave woman, blessed and favored by God. She had all the power in the world to succeed and obtain her heart's desire with the king.

So she donned her royal robes and told his officials, "Take me to the king!" As she went before the king unannounced, her heart raced as she awaited King Ahasuerus's response. If he expelled Queen Vashti from the palace for disobeying his orders, this act would surely get her into equal trouble. But just as before, Esther found favor in the eyes of the king. He didn't scold her or refuse her presence, but he welcomed her with open arms. He would grant whatever she wished. He acquiesced to her request of a dinner for Haman. Esther revealed to the king not only Haman's plan to kill all Jews but also that she was Jewish herself. He was greatly disappointed in the action of Haman and ordered his execution. The king couldn't stop the decree as affairs were set in motion. However, he was able to issue a counterdecree to protect the Jews from extermination. He allowed them to fight back and gifted them with Persian soldiers to fight alongside them. The victory and triumph of the Jews against the Persians is celebrated to this day during the festival of Purim.

Esther's story is one of beauty, devotion, intelligence, and courage. Her beauty got her into the palace, and her devotion led her to God for direction. Her intelligence led her to determine a plan securing the safety of her people, and her courage is what sealed the deal.

ENCOURAGEMENT EXERCISE: YEAR OF PREPARATION

At the dawn of a new year, everyone excitingly jumps to conjure up all of these great resolutions to lose weight, finish a degree, get a new house, obtain a certification—and the list goes on and on. But why wait until January 1? You can start your new you at any time of the year.

In Esther's story, we learned that in order to go before the king, the women were asked to prepare for a full year with oils, perfumes, potions, and creams. This was all done to ensure they were "perfect" in going before the king. In this encouragement exercise, we will explore preparing yourself to go before the King of Kings. If you were able to meet God within a year, how would you prepare yourself to go before Him? What would you improve for yourself?

First, identify at least six areas in your life that you would like to improve. This can be areas of weakness like excessive drinking, cursing, or gossiping or even thinking, speaking, and acting negatively toward people. Ask yourself: What are the areas in my life that are preventing me from having an elevated relationship with God?

After identifying these areas, assign a month (or more if you have fewer than twelve areas) in which you will actively work on improving each. Place the improvement areas on your calendar in the month in which they are assigned to keep you on track. Find a family member or friend to serve as your accountability partner, someone to whom you can report who will keep you honest with your progress. Over a twelve-month period, you will become an even greater you, a more polished version of yourself, as you prepare to go before the King.

Let's begin your year of preparation!

ON THE ROAD CALLED I-10: THE REASON

On the road of I-10, where life can also have its tragic end,
the road that took a young innocent life,
left a mother wondering, "Why did You burden me with such strife?"
Even as her friend, I couldn't help her find a suitable answer
to soothe her soul, to cure her heart's cancer.
In my talk with God, I said, "Four years on this earth is just not enough time.
How can this tragedy be a part of Your design?"
Then His answer to me made all the more sense,
and I've never questioned His divine design hence.
"My daughter, I am the I am, where life begins,
and true purpose has always been fulfilled when it ends."
This time on I-10 is where my unwavering trust in God begins.
My belief in God matured into total trust from within.
Trust that where you are in space and time,
even when you feel you are late, delayed, or behind,
is just where He wants you to be. This is not a crime.
When the truck flipped down the hill over ten times,
God had a bigger plan for me and my girls and left us behind.
What I thought as an inconvenience to my plan
is how God continued to keep us safe in His hands.
Nevermore do I worry when I feel interrupted in life,
for I trust He is protecting me from further strife,
for I am at peace and restin' in His arms.
He will always protect and keep me safe from harm.

This reflection on I-10 is where my trust in God matured. I experienced a tragic, horrific experience in which my friend's four-year-old daughter was taken from this earth. She perished in a car accident in which all others were spared. I knew that with this one fact that there was a lesson for me. I first turned to the logic of physics to gain understanding. I was assured that all the other passengers—a mom and two sons—were spared because their body mass created an equal and opposite force large enough to sustain them in their seats and prevent them from flying in the air. In my mind, this logic didn't hold valid against the fact that the vehicle flipped more than ten times down an incline of the highway. How was just one, a beautiful baby girl, taken? Why were the others spared? And furthermore, why did my daughters and I miss the ride? We were supposed to be in that vehicle.

I remember like it was yesterday receiving the call from the hospital informing me that they had three individuals with her and not four. The nurse stated, "Ma'am, I regret to inform you that the little girl did not survive." Time stopped; my heart sank into the pit of my stomach. I couldn't quite understand what the nurse was saying. It was as if she spoke a foreign language, not even born of this earth. I heard what she said clearly, but my head and my heart refused to comprehend what she stated. As I gathered myself, I immediately went into support mode, traveling the seventy miles to where those who had survived were being cared for. During that drive, I asked God to provide me guidance to understand the tragedy I was experiencing. He directed my thoughts from tragedy to treasure. He reminded me that He was still on the throne and thus still in control. I should not hang my head in sorrow but lift my hands and rejoice. For when anyone is taken away from this earth, He is waiting on them in heaven with open arms. This is not a tragedy but is God's providence.

He then reminded me how I had plans to travel to San Antonio for my daughter's cheer competition. Since my friend also had to travel to San Antonio, we thought it would be more efficient and less costly to carpool together. You see, that was *our* plan, not *the* plan—God's plan. I was delayed from departing with her because my daughter had a mandatory practice scheduled at the last minute. When I received the news of a last-minute practice, I was upset, frustrated, and all of the above because I was delayed from my plan. How dare they interrupt my plan at the last minute? But it wasn't *they*; it was *He* Who orchestrated the delay. Because I was delayed, I was saved.

How many times have you been delayed in traffic and stressed that you are late? How many times have you felt inconvenienced by a change in plans? God has you exactly where you are supposed to be even if you are delayed in the slightest bit, whether it is because you realize after ten minutes that the curling iron didn't heat up because it was unplugged or that those pesky kids put on the wrong attire to go to church on Sunday morning. Do not be anxious about being late, for you will always be right on time. God's providence is your protection—you may be delayed to miss an accident or some other harm that you have now avoided. Be at peace, and rest in His arms, and know that He is in control.

THE NEW TESTAMENT

Chapter 9

WE'LL LEAVE THE LIGHT ON FOR YOU

MARY

BIBLE READING: MATTHEW, MARK, LUKE, AND JOHN
VIRTUE: ACCEPTANCE

Dear Sister,

*E*very mother remembers that very moment at the birth of her child when she was told, "Congratulations! You are the proud mother of a healthy—" I remember my moment being quite different. An angel visited me in the field to say, "Congratulations! You are the proud mother of the Savior of the world!" My immediate response was, "Excuse me? Come again?" I was filled with so many emotions all at once. I was excited, confused, and nervous. But most of all, I was truly humbled to be chosen to birth the Savior of the world, and I burst into song. When the excitement wore off, reality began to set in. This is when I began to inquire of the Lord, "God, why can't we just wait until after I'm married to Joseph? My family will disown me. Joseph won't marry me. I could be stoned to death for adultery!" In my intimate conversations with God for direction, He assured me that His timing was purposeful. I was chosen to mother the Savior of the world. When I visited my cousin Elizabeth, her unbridled joy gave me all the confirmation I needed to pursue the impossible.

My response to Him was yes. And with my yes, this simple act of acceptance, I was able to fulfill my purpose in this world. This purpose was as unique to me as my fingerprint. I owned this uniquely created purpose, but the journey in achieving this purpose was owned by God. Instead of lowering my head in shame, I held my head high. He gave me the seed of destiny, and I was called to govern. I was now given the ability to see because of the seed that He planted inside me. As a daughter of Eve, my body was fearfully and wonderfully made to carry the seed of destiny for those around us (Psalms 139:14). I had the ability to see the destiny of my dear Jesus as a young child, even before He was able to see it in Himself. As His mother, I was able to see that He was the key to take us from religion to relationship with God. Through His walk, He would bring revelation. Through His resurrection, He would break the chains of rules and regulations. My act of acceptance brought access to the world.

My unconditional acceptance didn't mean that I would have a perfect journey. However, my unconditional acceptance meant that God would guide my journey. He gave me strength that I didn't even know I had to endure the four-day, one-hundred-mile journey from Nazareth to Bethlehem. He gave me confidence in my actions because my steps were ordered by His Word. The visit with my cousin Elizabeth was by His design. The timing of the Roman census that led us back to Joseph's hometown was by His design. And me, the unwed mother, being chosen as the vessel to shine the greatest Light of the world was by His design.

As the time came to deliver the Savior to the world, people would not take us into their homes. Instead of responding with "Do you know who I am?" I kept mum because I was kept in perfect peace by God. He then whispered to me, "We'll leave the light on for you." It was at this moment that I knew that God had just the perfect place for my darling Jesus to be born.

Hallelujah,
Mary

THE BROKEN VESSEL

Everyone should see Who is in us. Our light comes from the illumination of the Word inside us. We should never dampen this light to make others feel comfortable. Light energy travels in a straight line and allows us to see. When light reaches an object, some light is reflected, and this is what allows us to see the object. It is a proven fact that light located inside an object can only shine through an exposed area. A broken vessel serves as the perfect conduit for light to peer through.

God chose the Virgin Mary, whom many at her time considered broken, as the vessel to shine the greatest Light of the world: our Lord and Savior Jesus Christ. In her community, she must have been looked down upon as the rumored woman who had stepped out on her husband. Her fiancé, Joseph, even bought into this rumor, as he initially thought she must have gotten pregnant from someone else. He knew that he hadn't consummated the marriage, because at that time, the official ceremony had not taken place. Put plainly, there wasn't a marriage to consummate. I can only imagine the side eyes and whispers, and if the women in her time had pearls around their necks to clutch, they would have. But Mary was proud of the journey and the anointing that God had put on her life. And so should we be. Your life, your story, is not for those who are judgmental; it is not for the faint of heart. Your journey in life is for the glory of God.

The unbelievable strength of Mary at such a young age was remarkable. God was using Mary to display His promise that He will provide for all of our needs. Joseph was required to return back to his hometown for the Roman census. This ninety-seven mile, four-day journey on foot had to be quite the exhaustive journey for the pregnant Mary. Many of us who have been blessed to be pregnant can remember how traveling long distances can be a challenge. Shucks, just walking to your car can become quite the exhaustive journey. Can you imagine having to travel by donkey from Nazareth to Bethlehem?

Then after giving birth to the Savior, she still had quite the journey ahead of her. Once Herod was made aware that the three Magi were in search of the newly born King of Kings, he became jealous and ordered the death to all baby boys. This led Mary and Joseph to flee to Egypt to protect Jesus. Finally, when the coast was clear, and Jesus was of age to be hidden in plain sight, they returned to Nazareth and raised Him as a Nazarene. Even with this many concerns so early on in God's assignment for her life, she still yielded and accepted His call with glee.

REAL STORIES, REAL DELIVERANCE

The Bible is full of real stories of real women, and we can grow from what they have sown. I've always found comfort in the story of Mary because there are many parallels between her story of acceptance and my own. I learned that motherhood equals selflessness very early in my journey. By God's grace, I had just completed my high school experience as a top-four graduate from the largest high school in the state; I was an all-star athlete, a scholarship recipient, and a future engineer. Now in college, I found that the time had flown by quickly as I arrived at my sophomore year. I found myself in my third semester of college and pregnant, and my heart filled with dozens of emotions all at once. With many more questions than answers, I quietly contemplated to myself. "How did I make this mistake? What will people think of me with my dirty little secret? But I am still just a child myself…" The world's advice to what they considered my major faux pas was that I only had two choices to make, the two *a*'s: adoption or abortion.

Being encouraged by Mary's story, I knew there was a third *a*. As a believer, I knew in my heart there was only one choice: acceptance —acceptance of the path God had created for me and the blessing that He bestowed upon me. This was my first step toward my destiny; this key step of innate selflessness was instinctual. As a reward for my acceptance, God delivered my perfect Christmas gift to me at the perfect time. He created a timetable in which her birth coincided perfectly with my school's break, so much so that I didn't have to miss a single semester of school. With God's grace and mercy, I was able to not only survive college as a young mother, but I thrived.

People to this day still say to me, "Latoya, I don't know how you did it." When I am asked this question, I'm always reminded of a quote by Dr. Maya Angelou. It says, "Whatever is human is not alien to me." Basically, whatever any other human can do, you can do as well. I wasn't the first to be a young mother, and graduate from college. If they could do it, so could I. So I laced up my Nike sneakers and said "Just do it!" God's grace and mercy was sufficient for me.

Earlier in my life than I expected, I had to accept God's calling to be a mother. I was called to be a governess for His most precious blessing: life. I was fearful of attending church because God forbid I take the selfless route and give birth to a child of my own. I was scared to go to my family for solace because I was ashamed of continuing the generational "curse" of being a young mother that I had fought so hard to change. God forbid I walk around campus with a belly unwed. I was shunned by those closest to me at college because God forbid I serve as president and represent a one-hundred-year-old sorority as an unwed mother. I was even penalized by my professor for my choice as he gave me a failing grade in the most critical course of our engineering curriculum. God forbid I think I could finish a mechanical-engineering degree and be with child. God forbid I do the unexpected. But! God! God always delivers on the unexpected from us so that He can show His glory.

But what I realized is that I should never fear one individual in my life. The only One Who mattered was my Lord and Savior Jesus Christ, Who continues to provide me with His love and protection. He remains my guiding light, and He aligns my heart, mind, and soul to know that this was His journey for me and that my blessing, my beautiful daughter, will be such a blessing to this world. All I could muster with the strength I had left to go on was this: "The Lord is my light and my salvation, whom shall I fear, the Lord is the strength of my life, of whom shall I be afraid" (Psalms 27:1). As I prepared to walk across the stage during my commencement ceremony, I spotted the professor who had given me the failing grade. I walked up to him, shook his hand, and said, "You didn't think I would make it here, did you?" That statement wasn't just for him. To me, he represented everyone who had doubted God's providence. Not only did I finish college and obtain my degree without skipping a beat, but I was also able to achieve another with a third on the way. My acceptance of God's call, my yes, turned into my destiny.

I'M EVERY MOTHER

Mary has been called many names throughout thousands of years: Virgin Mary, Blessed Mother, Madonna, and most of all, the Blessed Mother of Jesus. Yes, she was the mother to the Savior of the world, but she still was a mother just like any of us. She exhibited all of the quintessential qualities we exhibit as mothers. She was very proud of her son Jesus and of the fact that He could perform miracles. Just like we, as mothers, want our children to show off their talents, she wanted Jesus to show just what He could do. She wanted Him to turn water into wine at a wedding to show everyone what He could do. I can imagine her pushing Jesus in front of everyone, saying, "Come on, baby, show them that thing that you can do!" Because of her ability to see the greatness in her Son, believers were able to witness the first miracle of the Savior and experience many more to come.

Mary had to experience the ultimate pain that no mother should ever have to experience. She had to witness the mocking, execution, and agony of her Child as He died on the cross. The same people who had just received her Son a few days prior with palms and open arms were now the ones to turn their backs on Him and sentence Him to death. They were gracious to Him when He healed their infirmities, cast out their demons, and fed the multitude. But now, they placed on His head a crown of thorns, whipped Him with lashes, and nailed Him to the cross with thieves. As a mother, Mary felt that His pain was her pain. She bled as He bled. She hurt as He hurt. I can only imagine that when they placed the crown of thorns on His head, she grabbed her head in pain. As they nailed His feet to the cross, she fell to her knees and prayed to God for the deliverance of her Son. Like many of us would have done, she probably asked God, "Why does my Son have to bear this burden? Why does my Son have to go through so much pain? Can I bear His burden instead?"

I have many "mothers" who circle me and encamp all around me to lead me to my destiny: my earthly mother, my heavenly mother, my godmother, my "other mother," my career mother. And the list goes on and on. And what you need to determine is this: What kind of mother are you? God gives us the seeds of destiny for those whom we are called to govern. He has given us all as women the ability to see because of the seed that has been planted in us. Our bodies are physically made different than men's to carry the seeds of destiny of those around us. That's why we have the ability to see what people are destined to be before they can see it in themselves. How many times have you looked at your children or children that you have been called to govern and say, "You will be a ballerina when you grow up" (or a doctor, an engineer, or a teacher)?

It's because God has given us the seeds and the abilities to see. We must take these callings and that energy and impart into those around us. We must go to the throne and speak to the Lord on their behalf. Each time we go to the Lord, we are able to get closer to God. We will develop more of a spirit of discernment and more of a spirit of peace and patience. Because it will take all three to impart a destiny into your hardheaded children. Even when they veer off the paths that you know God has for them, you keep speaking life into them until they fulfill their destinies.

Whether our children are biological or by proxy, we are all called to be mothers to those around us. As a mother, you have been ordained by God to care for, nurture, and to govern. If you are the neighborhood mom, godmother, teacher—basically any female who gives of herself in a loving manner to children—you are called to greatness. As a mother, you have been anointed and appointed and prepared for such a time as this. Just like Mary, you should accept your calling and begin to sing, "I'm every mother! It's all in me. Everything you want done, baby—I do it naturally!"

MOTHER stands for the following:

* Motivator: You are encouraging and are the biggest and loudest cheerleader.
* Oxygen: You give life, breathe life, and speak life. Mothers are the lifelines and the ever-living oxygen supplies.
* Teacher: You understand difficult matters and have the ability to deliver instruction effectively. Mothers have the patience to ensure that it sinks in.
* Honorable: You complete work that should be honored every day. Mothers do so humbly, not looking for anything in return but the love from those around them.
* Evangelist: You are willing to witness in any situation. Mothers love to engage people and rejoice in sharing Christ and the Word that Christ has given them.
* Right: You lead children down the right paths, knowing the right words to soothe and knowing how to nurture.

ENCOURAGEMENT EXERCISE: ACCEPTANCE TREE

Acceptance to God's call will oftentimes come when you least expect it. What you will be asked to accept may be the more unpopular opinion, the more undesirable direction. But each time you accept God's call, you add another branch to your life's tree. The fruit of these branches will become your life's work, your gift to the world. With the roots of your life's tree planted on the solid ground of God's Word, your tree will be fruitful and will multiply.

I encourage each of you to create your life's tree. Grab a sheet of paper and a pencil. Draw a tree trunk with branches extending from the top. For those of you who would like to be more artistic, you can use construction paper, paint, or color pencils to create a more realistic tree. For those of you like myself who are still trying to find those artistic bones in their bodies, you can cheat and go to the Internet, search for a tree drawing that you like, print, and paste.

Find a quiet space, and set some time to meditate and think back over your life of the times in which you have been called to action, called to acceptance. Write each of these items on a single branch. Once you have identified your branches, brainstorm the fruit that came from each act of acceptance. When you have your completed tree, take a step back to admire your life's work, and thank God for being called, anointed, and appointed for His glory.

Chapter 10

PAST-PERFECT TENSE

SAMARITAN WOMAN

BIBLE READING: JOHN 4:1–28
VIRTUE: PERSEVERANCE

Dear Latoya,

I know that for you, the many labels that you wear can become overwhelming. You have so many responsibilities for each: wife, mother, business owner, daughter, sister, friend, and even divorcée. At times, you can feel suffocated by the responsibilities of each and feel that they are impeding upon your ability to reach your destiny. But it is because of these many labels and many responsibilities that you are actually moving toward your destiny because we know that "to whom much is given, much is required." I can relate to you as a divorcée and how you had to turn lemons into lemonade. Just like you, many in my community made the label of "divorcée" synonymous with pity, shame, and disgrace. And God forbid we decide to move on and begin life anew with another man—girl! With the help of God, we had to do all we could to turn this label into one of courage and perseverance.

I remember there was a time that you would still wear your wedding ring while at the grocery store with your daughters because you didn't want others to label you as a disgrace and a failure as a single mother. Even though you grew up in a household where the single-mother label was synonymous with strength, passion, and survival, you succumbed to what others perceived of many young black women—just another poor, unfortunate soul. I also felt the same way; I could no longer wear my bridal piece, so instead of going to the watering hole when all other women in the community went together as was customary, I waited to go alone around noon when I knew that no one else would be there. I wanted to hide my divorcée label and avoid the stares, shunning, and side eyes of those who looked down upon me.

But guess what? On the day that I met Jesus at the well, He broke all the rules by speaking to me in public, and He knew of everything in my past—that I was five times divorced, that I was living with a man to whom I was not married, and that I was a Samaritan. But the only label that mattered to Him was "child of God." When He first asked for a drink of water, I looked over my shoulder to see if there was someone else there standing behind me, and I thought "Are you talking to me?" But as He continued to speak, I knew at that moment that He was the man they called the Messiah. I was excited to know that grace and mercy would be mine. At the same time, I was a bit perplexed in that the great Savior and Redeemer Whom I had heard so much about had chosen me. A Samaritan? A woman? A divorcée? But because He chose me to deliver His good news, this gave me all the strength and courage to run back to my community and let them know that I had met the Living Water at the watering hole. I wanted them to know that grace and mercy could be theirs if only they believed. So I encourage you, my sister, to remember that those against you do not have a heaven, nor hell, nor jail cell for you! Continue to wear your labels of warrior woman and child of God, continue to live your life as a conqueror, and continue to spread the good news!

Sincerely,
Samaritan Woman

OUR QUILT, THE MAKER, AND THE LABEL CREATOR

In the large collection of labels, labels can be neutral, positive, or negative. Daughter, sister, mother, wife—these are neutral labels that denote your interrelationship with another human. I believe that your neutral labels are all intrinsic qualities given to you at birth. Just as God is number-ing the hairs on your head, He is also creating your labels (Psalms 139:16). And yes, you read that correctly—I said wife! To be called to be a wife is a divine calling in His kingdom. If you believe you have been blessed with this anointing, don't wait to start walking in your anointing; walk now. Carry yourself as a wife in your thoughts, words, and deeds—your Adam will find you because he that finds a wife finds a good thing (Proverbs 18:22). God knows whether or not you will be a wife in your lifetime. He knows that you are just a lady-in-waiting for your Adam.

YOUR ANOINTING
Anointing is defined rubbing with oil as part of a religious ceremony in order to ceremonially confer divine office upon. Your anointing is bestowed upon you at birth, but it is up to you when you choose to walk in that anointing.

Then, the positive and negative labels are given to you by others and are based solely on an event or on the perception of how others feel you responded to the stimulus of that event. Positive labels include the following: smart, strong, kind, go-getter, trustworthy, creative, etc. Conversely, negative labels include the following: weak, divisive, narcissistic, untrustworthy, etc. When events occur during our lifetimes, there is a 50/50 chance that at the onset, the labels attached will be either positive or negative.

Let's take the Samaritan woman as an example. In the Bible, we are not given her name as we have been with many other women of the Bible, but it is very poignant that we are provided with her label: Samaritan. The Samaritans are a mixed race of people; Jews intermarried with the Assyrians who resettled Jewish land after torturing and sending them to exile around 722 BC. They were rejected by Jews as spiritual heretics and not accepted into the faith, even though they believed in God. They were against the rebuilding of the walls around the capital of Jerusalem in 445 BC that were torn down by the Babylonians. They observed the laws of Moses and worshiped on Mount Gerizim, the "hill of blessing," which is where Moses told the Jews to read God's promises of blessing after they entered Canaan.

People spoke death over her because of the past of her people and her personal past. But because she believed in the Son of God, she had life (1 John 5:11–13). He spoke life over her, and her past became the perfect tense for her to reach her destiny, which was to become an evangelist for the Redeemer, our Lord and Savior Jesus Christ!

THE SAMARITAINS-THREE STRIKES YOU'RE OUT!
The Samaritans were shunned by the Jews for three key reasons: (1) they revered only an edited form of the first five books of the Bible; (2) they were against the rebuilding of the walls; and (3) they worshiped on Mount Gerizim.

I can just imagine her after she met Jesus at the well. She confidently ran back to town, asked everyone to gather in the town square, and told them she had a special message from the Lord and Savior to deliver. She had them captive, ready to hang on her every word. And with her hands on her hip, waving her index finger, she began to recite the words from Marvin Sapp's ballad "Best in Me" with sass and confidence:

> *He saw the best in me*
> *when everyone else around*
> *could only see the worst in me.*
> *See, He's mine, and I am His.*
> *It doesn't matter what I did.*
> *He only sees me for who I am.*

When we have a special encounter with God, we have been blessed to experience a miracle. It is our duty as believers to spread the good news just as the Samaritan Woman did.

I believe that who you are is a manifestation of your past events—all of the good, the bad, and the ugly. As a wife, mother, sister, daughter, or career woman, who you are shows up when faced with adverse situations. Who you are even shows up when you least expect it in those small moments when you reach out your hand to introduce yourself.

My dear sisters, don't be ashamed of your pasts, but own them. Your past experiences mend together like a patchwork quilt. The labels build this quilt that you will have to fall back on when you go through adverse situations. This is the quilt that will be there to catch you when you should have chosen door number 2 but instead chose number 1. It is the quilt that will comfort you and give you the strength to persevere when you endure hardships—the quilt that, when life tends to not look to be in your favor, helps you to continue boldly until the ship turns around. You know that God is the ultimate Label Creator and Quilt Maker, and He will reward your perseverance openly.

One of the most important patches of my quilt is to always have a positive outlook. I always state in my bio that I come from humble beginnings. This is a very polite way to say that we were broke as a joke and oftentimes didn't have two pennies to rub together. Forget the thought of having your own room; I couldn't even entertain the idea of having my own bed until I was twelve, and I mostly shared a bed with either my grandmother or mother. Although I felt shame at the time because of what we could and couldn't afford, I now realize that the blessing was in the moment, that I had a bed to sleep in and that I could share and gain even more intimate nurturing from those loved ones around me. Instead of wearing a negative label of pessimism and running around saying, "The world will always be difficult for someone like me," I decided to wear the positive label of optimism. It's a very valuable lesson that I take into business, and I pursue every opportunity with patience and perseverance. There is always a positive in every moment.

During my first internship with Texaco oil company, other interns had their own cars, or their parents owned cars, and they could be dropped off. Although the office was a mere fifteen-minute drive away from my home, I had to wake up every morning at 4:30 a.m. to ensure my prompt 7:00 a.m. arrival. My grandmother would serve as my protector and walk me to the bus stop with her walking stick to ward off the unsavories. I would ask her, "Big Ma, who is gonna protect you as you walk home?" Her answer would always be, "Ain't nobody gonna bother me with this big stick and God on my side!" She knew that I was still maturing in my walk with God and needed her earthly protection. But her faith in His heavenly protection was firmly solidified, and she knew the angels of grace and mercy walked by her side and would protect her all the way back home. Although I felt shame at the time because my arrival was different than the other interns who would drive up in their nice cars or with their parents driving them, I continued to press forward and pursue this blessing from God.

As I strengthened my faith in God, I turned this label of shame into one of tenacity. By the next summer's internship, I was able to purchase my own car and drive myself to my new internship—now more than three times the distance farther. You see, this was God's test to see if I could be faithful with minimal resources despite the obstacles that I had with getting there. He was preparing me for what was even bigger and greater to come: the newer internship, which was the start of my personal journey of spiritual growth along I-10. In looking back, I reaped a valuable life lesson in all that was sown. It doesn't matter how you get there as long as you arrive and take your seat at the table that God has prepared for you. Getting there is your first step to greatness, just as it was with the Samaritan woman. It didn't matter how she got to the well, as long as she arrived and took her place in history as God's anointed.

ENCOURAGEMENT EXERCISE: LIFE QUILT

Efficacy is defined as the potential that is available to produce a desired result. Your personal efficacy is the potential you have inside of you to achieve your goals, your destiny. Efficacy is a sum total of your qualities built from your past experiences—your confidence, your value system, and your obstacles. It is what makes you, *you*!

This exercise will help you explore the following: What are the qualities and characteristics of you, the reader? What in your past impacts your relationship with God and your view of yourself? With the answers to these questions, you will begin to build your quilt—your embroidery of efficacy.

I encourage each of you to begin weaving your quilt. Find your quiet place, and take a few moments to identify and write down the first three patches that come to mind—three events in your life's journey in which you showed courage, resiliency, or perseverance. Take fifteen minutes to expound upon these moments that will help you move closer to understanding the efficacy needed to achieve your destiny. Each subsequent week, set aside time to identify at least one more patch of your quilt, one more instance in which God saw your past as the perfect tense. Don't place your quilt behind a "break in case of emergency" glass. Instead, be sure to share and share often with others. These "aha moments" give you deference to your past, provide agility in your present, and give you laser focus for your future.

Chapter 11

MARY DON'T YOU WEEP; MARTHA, PUT THOSE DISHES DOWN!

MARY AND MARTHA

BIBLE READINGS: LUKE 10:38-41; JOHN 11:1-44; AND JOHN 12:1-7

VIRTUE: WORSHIP

Dear Sister,

There comes a time in every woman's life when she has to learn to simply put the dishes down. And when I say "put the dishes down," I mean that the word "dishes" can be replaced with anything that is a distraction in your life—cell phone, laptop, unwashed clothing. It includes anything and everything that represents our daily obligation of all the neutral labels we wear as wives, mothers, teachers, business owners, and the like. We can become so overly focused on upholding these unattainable standards that "they" have set—"they" always have something to say. Has anyone every figured out who "they" are? Ha!—that we miss living in the moment and being able to recognize what is important in that moment. So for me, I've always held on tight to my label of big sister. As the elder woman of the house, I felt that the responsibility fell on my shoulders to take care of the needs of the house and the needs of my brother Lazarus and sister Mary.

We were in the midst of Hanukkah, when we celebrated the rededication of the temple built by King Solomon many years ago. This is when our dear brother Lazarus fell ill. Immediately, we sent word to Jesus to come and see about His friend. But oddly enough, His response was not immediate. This concerned me greatly. Every day that passed, I became more and more worried that He had not arrived. I thought, surely, if He can deliver miracles to others, He can do this for one of His most loyal followers and trusted friend. So I went out looking for Him; He needed to know how heartbroken I was because it was too late. I told Him, "My brother has been dead for four days; he's gone, and his soul has left his body. Why do You still choose to come?" I couldn't believe that Mary just stayed behind and didn't want to give Him a piece of her mind as well. After all, she was such an avid believer that she had left me to tend to all the hostess duties when he and the gang of twelve came prior for Passover. I thought that Jesus favored her more than me. I thought she would have been even more disappointed than I.

But as Jesus spoke to me, it became clear that this was my moment, my moment for an intimate encounter with Him. His voice calmed my worries. He asked a simple question, the only question that truly mattered in this moment. He asked if I believed in Him and believed that whoever believes shall never perish but have everlasting life. This was my moment of conviction, and I uttered a single word: "Yes." In that moment, I didn't just secure my brother's salvation but also my own. In that moment, I went from a worry to worship of our Lord.

Warmly,
Martha

ONCE, TWICE, THREE TIMES THE LADY…WHO WORRIES

Martha is mentioned in the Bible three times, and in each of those three times, she is worried about one of her younger siblings. In Luke 10:38–42, Martha was worried that her sister was not helping her to serve when Jesus and the disciples stopped in for a rest from their journey. Jesus assured her that Mary was doing the most pertinent thing at the time, which was seizing the moment to be in the presence of God. Then, after Jesus did not arrive in time to heal their brother Lazarus, and he subsequently died, Martha was furious. Four days had passed, and Martha took it upon herself to go and meet Jesus to give Him a piece of her mind. She told Him that if He had been there in time, her brother would not have died. Even in her state of worry, she knew that she served a mighty God and that Jesus was the Great Connector. She told Jesus that whatever He asked of Him would be given. Now with Lazarus resurrected, the three of them chose to thank Jesus by hosting Him at dinner six days before Passover. Martha was still worried with the tasks of serving food but not serving Jesus. Her sister Mary once again sat at the feet of Jesus, but this time, she anointed Him with oil to honor Him as the Savior. Possibly she sensed His impending death on the cross, and there was no time like the present to revere Him.

Let's break down the word "worry." This word is derived from the Old English word "wyrgan," which means to choke or to strangle. This is very analogous to how worry can choke the life out of us, and how with our constant worrying, we can choke the life out of those around us. Worry is defined as having many bad thoughts with some fear and expending much time with these bad thoughts but not taking action on them. Anxiety, unease, and trouble lead to worry; shame, regret, and sadness lead to worry; hate, panic, and overthinking lead to worry. The use of the word "worry" in the English language has increased exponentially since 1970. In retrospect, this makes total sense since this is after the peace movements of the 1960s. From the 1970s forward, so many events in the world have compounded the fear factor and compounded confusion among many. These events serve as the perfect fertilizer for worry to grow.

The very existence of worry in my life is something that I battle to extinguish daily. I feel it is the biggest and most frequent act of sin that I execute against God. Yes, it is sin in that it breaks the first and greatest commandment: "Thou shall have no other gods before me." At times I can become so worrisome that it's like I'm worshipping at the altar of worry versus communing with God in His Holy Place. I've learned that when I focus on the immediate and not the farfetched, I can remain in perfect peace (Isaiah 26:3).

Jokingly, I always wondered of God's reaction when I would get all flustered and worried time and time again. I imagine it happens in this manner. God is standing in heaven with His arms folded, shaking His head, checking His watch as He waits on me. He's thinking, "When is she just gonna get out of the way? Doesn't she know that the sooner she gets out of the way, the sooner I can get to work? How many times do I have to show her that I've got it?"

I've personally tried to slow the physical manifestations of chronic worry on my body by taking prescribed medication. I thought this was my only recourse to stop the worry. But the pills would only mute the effects of worry for a short period of time. Then I began taking more pills just so I could sleep through the pain. I would wake up again the next day and do it all over again. Wash, rinse, repeat. Like many, what I failed to grasp was that taking the mind-altering pills could not stop life events from occur-ring. What I really needed to alter naturally was the way I reacted to the ups and downs of life.

As I've immersed myself in the Word, I've matured in my walk with the Lord, and my prayers—or as I like to call them, my conversations with the Lord—have evolved. I went from prayers of despair ("Lord, why?") to prayers of plea ("Lord, please!") to prayers of thanksgiving ("Lord, I just thank you!"). This is because my worries began to cease; the doubts and the thoughts of defeat began to cease and were replaced with peace, His peace that surpasses all understanding. In continual worship of Him I say, "You did not create me to worry. You did not create me to fear. But You created me to worship daily. So, Imma leave it all right here." Thank you Anthony Brown for the perfect words.

But as the increase in the usage of the word "worry" suggests, I'm not the only one with an invitation to the worry party. Just in my immediate circle, many of my family and friends experience severe bouts of worry. Even the strongest Christians will worry about things, ranging from whether a nuclear-terrorist attack is headed our way to whether the percentage of battery life left in a cell phone will be sufficient to make it to the charger that was left at home (because God forbid we miss a call, text, tweet, or snap). This worry manifests itself in our bodies as stress, and 25 percent of all Americans have recalled experiencing significant stress recently. They've cited symptoms such as loss of mental agility, eye twitching, hair loss, and even worry warts! If not managed effectively, these symptoms can lead to many adverse-health risks including chronic fatigue, intestinal problems, chronic pain, and even heart trouble.

After a scary trip to the emergency room with test after test to discern the origin of chest pains and the numbness in my arm, I knew for sure that more pills were needed. Even after I made a conscious decision to stop tak-ing the pills sometime prior, I felt like this was my only answer. Just as I began to text in my refill to the pharmacy (yes, they really make it too easy nowadays), the voice of God spoke through my doctor and told me, "You don't need those pills!" I initially looked up in a state of shock and won-dered, "How could the doctor know I was about to order pills at this very moment?" He proceeded to explain to me that I could keep paying him to run tests, and he could continue to prescribe pills. But I would be wast-ing my time and my money; it would all be for naught. In order for a true change in my state of health to occur, I would need to adjust my approach to life. Then, a state of peace rushed over me. I knew this was the hand of God letting me know that He had my back and that I could put down the pills for a life of peace in His arms.

STRESS

Stress is the body's response to the overload of worry and perceived challenges and threats to a person's well-being. Through stress, the body is preparing to face the danger that the individual is worried about.

THREE TYPES OF WORRIERS

There are three types of worriers—past, present, and future. Past worriers are extremely concerned with whether things from the past will repeat themselves. Correction—they have convinced themselves that these things surely will happen. Present worriers always see events or receive information presented to them through a negative filter. Future worriers concern themselves with flights of fancy and building stories of what may be. The "what-if" scenarios overcrowd their minds and cloud their judgments.

The enemy would have us to think that if we worry about a loved one, that means that we care about them. Conversely, we are tricked into thinking that if we don't worry, then we don't love them. This is not of God. Worry is not love. Many of you reading this may say, "But Latoya, my son is strung out on drugs; how am I not supposed to worry?" Worry is born of the human flesh, and worship is born of the spirit. My sister, my answer to you is this: "Will you or your worry be there to pull the needle out of his arm, the pipe out of his mouth, or the pills from his throat in that moment?" There is no guarantee to this. Depend on God; don't depend on what you can do only through your might. You are not God. Worship the only One who can do any of these things. As 1 Peter 5:7 states, "Casting all your care upon Him, for He cares for you." We've all heard the saying "Let go, and let God." But allow me to add this: "Pray, and get out of the way!" Let His grace and mercy flow, and the flow can only occur where worry does not exist.

I have news for us worrywarts: faith and worry cannot exist in the same body. Faith is synonymous with life and worry synonymous with death. Life and death cannot exist in the same place. When David was presented with battling Goliath, he was offered the shield by a fellow soldier. This soldier was worried about the young David being a conqueror because Goliath was a giant. However, David didn't flinch because he had faith that God was there for him in his previous fights. His size didn't matter, and the worries of those around him didn't matter. David knew that this fight was no different than the others in which God had given him the victory (1 Samuel 17). Daniel was not worried in the lion's den because he was anchored in faith in that God was in control. The three Hebrew boys were not worried about stepping into the fiery furnace because they knew this was the time for God to show even nonbelievers that He was in control. Their faith left them unscathed with not even one thread of their garments being charred (Daniel 3:8–30). Faith will win over worry every time. The question we must all ask ourselves is this: "Which one am I allowing to win?"

ENCOURAGEMENT EXERCISE: PIE TEST

Over the years, I've attended several conferences, and each would have at least one workshop dedicated to achieving life balance. In those workshops, the participants are typically asked to draw a pie chart that represents their daily time allocations. They are asked to identify the percentages of time in their days that are spent on themselves, their kids, spouses, etc. My only problem with this approach is that we typically use a broad brush to determine how we spend our time, and there may be a bit of hedging due to our own perceptions.

I encourage each of you to take this pie-chart activity one step further. Start with taking a true account of one complete day, and capture the amount of time you spend on each activity to within the quarter of an hour (fifteen minutes). Identify into which category each activity falls: self, spouse, kids, work, family, and friends. Determine the percentages, and create the pie chart. Assess your chart, and ask yourself the following: Am I spending enough time on myself? Am I living my ideal balanced life? If not, where can I make adjustments? Create a plan to make adjustments you need to reduce worry and achieve peace.

ON THE ROAD CALLED I-10: THE REBIRTH

On the road called I-10 is where my rebirth commenced,
the true connection of all five senses.
My destiny before me and now in my grasp,
I would become of Him what I asked.
My words would now be shared with the world,
used as words of wisdom, treasured as pearls.

On the road called I-10 is where my rebirth began. It is now almost twenty years later, and I find myself older, wiser, and kinder—just a tad bit. I was offered a contract in this small town outside of Baton Rouge, Louisiana. Plant life was in my view once again along I-10! I had the opportunity to reconnect with that which I knew, traveling I-10 to take me back to my roots, of which I am proud: my college; my church home; and my sorority. These places are where I learned how to be the best Latoya I could be. But those connections were all secondary; they were ancillary compared to the reconnection to my destiny.

I found myself pregnant again during my encounter with I-10. But this time, I was ready to give birth to my destiny as an author. I have been pregnant in the spirit with this book for years but could never bring it to full term because I wasn't nourishing my mind and soul as one is supposed to nourish her body during pregnancy. To nourish, I would listen to sermons by various preachers and listen to my audio Bible with an intent to truly understand, and this is where this book was born.

As I began to get more into the Word, all hell began to break loose in my life like never before. My godmother, Janice, kept encouraging me, explaining that all of these crazy happenings were confirmations that I was on the right track. It was imperative that I press forward along my journey on I-10 to fulfill the calling that God had over my life. As I continued to press forward, I was at a loss for how I was going to complete the book. All of these distractions were zapping my energy and taking my focus off completing this book. Then I would receive additional encouragement from my writing coach to continue my journey. I am eternally grateful to her for serving as my midwife through this entire rebirth along I-10 and beyond.

Chapter 12
GREAT EXPECTATIONS

MARY MAGDALENE

BIBLE READINGS: MATTHEW 27:54–66; MATTHEW 28:1–10;
MARK 15:37–47; MARK 16; LUKE 8:1–3; LUKE 24:1–12
VIRTUE: BELIEF

Dear Blessed Believer,

God looks beyond the outside and knows it's the heart that matters. The disciples were a motley crew of tax collectors that were known to have shady business dealings, fishermen and seafaring men known to love 'em and leave 'em. They were known to use bad language at the drop of a dime. On the outside, they looked like a group of bad-news bears, but Jesus saw their hearts. When they arrived into town, they were looked down upon by our Pharisee leaders as being just followers of this crazy man—this crazy man with this crazy power who was breaking all the rules. I could see that they were changed men, and they now were men of purpose. Their potential energy was now kinetic because they were connected to the Source. As a leader, He took the ultimate sacrifice so that His team could rise to the next level, the level of apostles. They were hand selected by God for a true purpose, the purpose of spreading the good news throughout the world.

Matthew and Thomas were selected because as tax collectors, they would be able to handle the finances for the movement and ensure financial stability. The brothers James and John were fisherman who would become fishers of men. Since they were avid catchers of fish, now they could be catchers of men in the same way to follow Jesus and His teachings. Ironically, even Judas fit into the equation as he was a money changer, and ultimately his changing of money to betray Jesus for thirty pieces of silver was the catalyst to the crucifixion and then the Resurrection.

So it was the same for me; I was selected because I had seven demons, symbolizing a completeness of possession. Thus, I had the capacity for my mind to be occupied by a number of ideas at once. Once I was delivered by Jesus, my mind now had the capacity to be occupied by the teachings of the Greatest Who ever lived. In the end, I was the only disciple who could understand all of His teachings in their entirety. I went from completeness of possession to completeness of understanding.

Over the centuries, I have been called everything from a prostitute to an unrepentant woman—and everything in between. I could not get caught up in all of their name-calling from those who called themselves Christians. I simply ignored them and just shook my head. How can you call yourselves a Christian but do the exact opposite of what Jesus teaches by spreading falsehoods in an attempt to malign someones character? It didn't matter what they called me; I knew that I was called by God for His express purpose: to support His only begotten Son. I knew that in believing in Him, I would not perish but have everlasting life. My life and legacy would live on and stand the test of time. I knew that they would eventually get it right. It took almost twenty centuries, but finally they honored my story. And getting it right was not about me and personal gratification, but it was about empowerment of women like yourself to be leaders and do amazing things in His kingdom.

I'd heard of the many miracles of Jesus, from healing a multitude of their infirmities to raising a widow's son from the dead. I was particularly moved by the miracle of healing a man from an unclean demon in Capernaum. He commanded the unclean spirit to come from the man, and the spirit obeyed. This was fascinating, and I thought to myself, "Wow, He can even remove demons! He must be the key to my salvation." I was in great expectation of His arrival to our city. Surely, if I could be in the presence of the Holy One, if I could tap into His energy, then I could be saved from my life of demon possession. As He saved Joanna, Susanna, and myself, we felt forever indebted to Him, and we left our homes to become one of His disciples. Now a part of the movement, I was able to see firsthand the wonders of Jesus that had been chronicled from city to city and village to village. The sensitivity and compassion of how the Miracle Worker treated the woman with the issue of blood truly warmed my heart.

She had a lifelong infirmity that rendered her unclean and was condemned by rabbis from worshipping God. She'd been seen and treated by the best doctors in the land for over twelve years, but the issue of blood still remained. Relentless and hardheaded, she was determined to find a solution for her ailment. I saw her push through the crowd. I saw the determination in her eyes. She knew that even if she could only get to touch the hem of His garment that she would be healed. She tried to push with all of her might, but with such a large loss of blood, her physical strength was depleted. God showed up in the very moment when she was unsure whether she could make it to Him on her own. Because, you see, we are God's sheep, and just when we think we don't have much more to give and can't go any further, and when all strength is gone, He picks us up and carries us over the finish line. God carried her to the feet of Jesus so that she could tap into the Source. He could feel the energy transfer from His body and looked around to find out who was the recipient. Instead of rebuking her, He called her "daughter," and immediately she obtained true healing. She had spent several years trying to use resources to heal her, but it wasn't until the single moment that she tapped into the Almighty Source that she was able to be freed from her ailment. By touching His hem, she completed the energy circuit. Then and only then was His healing power able to flow freely from His body.

The energy of the Almighty can neither be created nor destroyed, but it can be passed to us. The catalyst for this energy transfer is simply our belief in the Almighty and in His everlasting power. Once I believed, I received, and then I was ultimately able to cleave to my purpose and was free to pursue my destiny.

Live by the Word, and die by the Word,
Mary

THE VIRTUOUS WOMAN

It was difficult to select a single virtue to encapsulate all that is Mary Magdalene because she embodies all of the other virtues we've explored in this book. As an evangelist, she accepted God's call and showed her faith to His only begotten Son. She exhibited loyalty and possessed the courage to remain at the foot of the cross, risking arrest for being connected to Jesus when mostly all others had deserted Him for fear of persecution. Her love for Jesus was unconditional and everlasting as she waited until He breathed His last breath. She showed her obedience to God by acknowledging Jesus as His Chosen Messiah. She waited patiently for answers at the tomb when she saw that the stone was rolled away and the body was gone. She was in complete servitude to the Lord and made His mission and His life her priority. Through her followship of Jesus and His teachings, she became a leader and an apostle for the Christian faith. She trusted the sovereignty of the Lord in that He can be of Himself to send Himself in human form to worship Himself. Most of all, Mary was a radical believer. She believed in the incorruptible, infallible Word of God. She believed that Jesus was the Savior of the world.

With the removal of the demons that possessed her mind, body, and spirit, she was now able to have the Lord enter in. After Jesus delivered her from her demons, she could have gone about her way. Instead, she left her home and dedicated her life to Christ. This was radical for a woman to do at this time. Mary was free to live a life as a disciple of Christ. There was freedom and liberation in living in God's truth and His Word. The world would make you think that freedom is being led by your own mind and doing what you want to do. However, it's truly about having a renewed mind through the teachings of God and a freedom in living in His truth (John 8:31).

The seven demons blocked her ability to receive the good news. Now she was open to not only receive the good news, but to spread the gospel of Christ to others. She took her role in the movement very seriously as a nurturer in providing for the disciples. She was not just a leader among the female brood of believers, but she was seen as Jesus's right hand, right up there with Peter. She felt forever grateful to the man Who saved her life. He saved her from a life of bondage to demons to a life of freedom in the teachings of Jesus, her Savior, her Rabbi, her Lord.

Many of the virtues of Mary are not provided for in our traditional Bible. This is mainly because of centuries upon centuries of decisions to determine which gospels would be included in the Bible. These decisions could have been skewed by the misogyny of male church leaders in the fourth century. Lost biblical texts called the Gnostic gospels were found in 1945 in Egypt and provide a more detailed picture of the importance of Mary in Christian history. They include the Gospel of Thomas, the Gospel of Phillip, and the Gospel of Mary, among others. In all of these gospels, Mary had the most prominent role as an apostle. Jesus trusted her and Peter most of all with even His most precious of teachings. Of all the disciples, she was the only one to completely understand the teachings of Jesus. Her completeness of possession was now transformed to a completeness of understanding—so much so that He would teach her in private sessions, and she would receive special lessons that were not given to others. The texts also state that she was Jesus's most loved and trusted confidant. It is thought that these gospels were not included in the Bible in order to solidify the sainthood of Peter over Mary by early church leaders. Although the authenticity of these gospels and their inclusion in biblical history are debated, the fact still remains that she was an integral part in the foundation of Christianity.

MARY MAGDALENE: BC

The life of Mary Magdalene, BC—Before she met Christ—has baffled Bible scholars for years. This woman of mystery was also an agent of change for the Christian movement. Some have called her an apostle, some the woman with the jar of alabaster, and some have even called her a prostitute. Her origin has even been debated—was she from the town of Magdala? Or was she a woman of African origin who came to Jerusalem to learn of this great man that they called Jesus of Nazareth? Even her relationship with Jesus has been ultimately sensationalized in the blockbuster hit *The Da Vinci Code*. As Jesus's most loved disciple, was she also His wife and the mother of His child? Even though all of these characteristics of Mary are still debated to this day, an undeniable fact still remains—she was an integral part in the foundation of Christianity.

When Jesus met Mary Magdalene, she was with a group of other women who were possessed with a legion of demons. This legion of demons most likely included some of the disorders that we battle with today: anxiety, depression, and low self-esteem. In the gospels of Matthew, Mark, and Luke, those who were possessed with demons were said to have afflictions such as speechlessness, violence, blindness, convulsions, and foaming at the mouth. With wide eyes and with hair disheveled, I can only imagine that these women were rendered undesirable and placed in a separate location away from the community like trash. But what others saw as trash, He saw as treasure. Jesus healed these women of their afflictions and restored them to their paths of greatness. These women became followers of Jesus as He spread the good news. With Mary at the helm, the women provided for those involved in the movement from their own personal resources.

This prominent woman of the Bible has been a source of mystery for centuries because very few details of her life are given in the Bible. But what we do know of her origin is that that she was from a town called Magdala, meaning "tower or castle." Its location on the shore of the Sea of Galilee elevated the town of Magdala to a level of importance in the region as a fishing and trade center. We can only infer that she was unmarried with no children because as we are introduced to various persons of the Bible, they are named and connected to either their spouses, their children, or other family members. She was named in the Bible as Mary of Magdalene and connected to her city of origin, similar to how Jesus was named Jesus of Nazareth. Her singleness can also be confirmed in knowing that she was able to leave home and move around freely with Jesus and the other disciples. The only characteristics that we know before she met Jesus are the following: she was from Magdala, was demon possessed, and was unmarried. So why do some refer to her as a prostitute or an unrepentant, wayward woman before she met Jesus?

This connection of Mary to a woman of sexual proclivity came from assumptions made by early church leaders. Nowhere in the gospels does it state that she was a promiscuous woman. However, she was assumed to be the woman with the alabaster box of oil who wiped the feet of Jesus with her tears. Since this unnamed woman and Mary were introduced back-to-back in the text of Luke, over time, these two became one individual. Also as evidence to support their claim, Magdala was known as a town of many prostitutes. However, being that Magdala was a seafaring town, this was not a difficult connection to make as it is very common for seafaring towns even to this very day to have women of the night to greet the men who would come after spending many days out at sea. But just because she was from the town doesn't mean that she was of it. In the third century, church leaders solidified their claims by calling her the "penitent Mary." To further add insult to injury, her seven demons were connected to the seven deadly sins, with lust being the primary one. She became the promiscuous woman whom Jesus saved from a life of sexual immorality.

However, there is not even a grain of evidence to support these claims. These claims fit the third-century leaders' need at the time to put women in their place and discourage them from serving as leaders by diminishing the character of Mary. God forbid women believe they can serve! Then in the sixth century, Pope Gregory I declared her as a fallen woman guilty of forbidden acts and lumped Mary Magdalene, Mary of Bethany, and the unnamed woman in as one. Finally, this negative connotation was removed by Pope Francis IV in 1969, which helped to restore Mary to her rightful place as a key founder and leader of the Christian movement.

Throughout the Bible, we have seen God use even the least, those discarded by society, for His greatness. Rahab was a prostitute, but she was still the key to unlocking the Promise Land for the Israelites. So it is not a problem if Mary Magdalene was a prostitute. However, falsehoods should not be used to create a cultural bias toward an individual simply in order to achieve the misogynistic goals of ensuring that church leaders are only men.

THE CATALYST

It is a scientific fact that potential energy can only turn into kinetic after being acted upon by some sort of effort or push. For example, a ball sitting at the top of a cliff has a great potential energy in proportion to its size. A catalyst is needed to activate the energy; otherwise, the ball would just sit there. Then, once pushed, this energy converts into kinetic energy as it falls to its resting place at the ground below. It is a spiritual fact that you have the same amount of potential that you've always had since birth. God placed your promise inside of you at the time of your arrival on earth. God is also the Catalyst Who will activate our potential to turn it into kinetic energy. You must tap into the energy Source in order to arrive at your destiny. In order to tap into God's power, you will be asked to complete an action. I like to call this the catalytic event, which is the pivotal point in which God can release His unbelievable blessings. For every action, there is an equal and opposite reaction. And that action is multiplied when we allow God to serve as the Catalyst.

As an example, in the story of the feeding of the multitude with five fish and two loaves of bread, we are shown that God served as the

Catalyst when Jesus looked up to heaven and blessed the fish and loaves and then broke them. He then commanded not only the multitude to sit in groups but asked the disciples to complete an action as well. This is the catalytic event that would allow them to tap into God's power and turn their potential energy into kinetic. What they didn't know is that they possessed the potential all along to bless the multitude and were designed for such a time as this. When the disciples complied and did what was requested of them from Jesus, the conversion from potential to kinetic occurred. Obeying God's request was the catalytic event that allowed the Catalyst to multiply the blessing. Through the Catalyst, the fish and loaves of bread placed in their hands were multiplied to feed not just one family but to also feed the multitude. And it was well over five thousand individuals who left with full bellies and happy plates. Five thousand is the number that only identifies the men who were present, but if you account for women and children, you can easily arrive at ten thousand or more who were fed. Because they obeyed His action, they were blessed.

Another great example of this catalytic process in action is the story of the man who had an infirmity that prevented him from walking for thirty-eight years (John 5: 1–9). Jesus found the man lying at the pool of Bethesda on a porch. The pool of Bethesda was known at this time for having healing properties, and this is why he and many others were sprawled around its five porches. Jesus knew that the man had lain there in despair for quite some time. He had to inquire whether he still was interested in being healed or if he wanted to stay in his immobile state. The man responded with several excuses of why he'd never made it to the healing waters. Excuse number one: No one would help him there. Excuse number two: When he finally makes it close, someone always jumps in front of Him. I can only imagine that a confused look came over Jesus's face, and He thought once again, "Does this man want to be healed?" Then Jesus commands the man to take up his bed and walk. As soon as he did what the Lord commanded, he was able to walk after thirty-eight years of being paralyzed. This catalytic event was the key to his healing. He led him beside the still waters of the Bethesda and restored his soul (Psalms 23:2).

MARY MAGDALENE: AD.

Jesus activated the potential that resided in Mary. The demons that possessed Mary served as an insulator to her energy and muted her power. Once she tapped into the energy Source, she was liberated. She was free to walk in her purpose and serve Christ in His movement, crucifixion, and resurrection. She did not just want to be a Christian in private or when it was convenient. With her energy now kinetic, her passion for her beliefs was electric.

The Bible tells us that she was there at three critical times in the last moments of Jesus on this earth. She was the last to remain at the cross during the crucifixion. All other disciples had deserted Him, and she looked around and wondered where their devotion was. But she waited patiently to hear her Lord state, "It is finished!" She was the first to visit His tomb and discover that the stone had been rolled away and that no body remained. She ran to tell the other disciples, and upon seeing just the grave clothes with not a body in sight, they left and went back home in despair. Mary remained at the Garden of Gethsemane. She was the only one to show patience and resilience and refused to leave until she saw her Lord. Because of her devotion, she was the first person to witness Jesus after His resurrection. At first, she mistook Him for the gardener. As she moved closer, He spoke her name, and she realized it was her Lord and Savior and immediately shouted, "Rabbi!" She could see only because she believed. And it was her belief that led her to continue her discipleship for Christ.

We know that God does things according to His design and in decency and in order. With a specificity and a purpose, He chose Mary Magdalene as the person to witness His crucifixion and His resurrection. It is not by chance that He chose a woman to witness the two foundational moments that established the modern-day Christian faith. After reading Mary Magdalene's story, questions still remain: What was God's purpose in selecting this woman of questionable origin as His witness? Why is she not celebrated more for her importance in establishing the Christian faith? Why isn't this woman honored with a more prominent position in Christianity?

ENCOURAGEMENT EXERCISE: REFLECTION

Along our journey, we have explored twelve virtues of twelve amazing women. As we disembark, I would like our final exercise to be one of reflection. Take a moment to reflect on your past as a broken woman, an anointed woman, a woman of virtue. In your passport journal, identify how you have displayed each of the virtues in the past and how you will display this virtue in the future.

Then capture each of the twelve virtues on a Post-it Note, and place the notes around your home, your office, your car, or any personal space you may visit during the day. Use the notes to speak a word over yourself and provide yourself with encouragement and empowerment. You are fearfully and wonderfully made in His image, a daughter of the great "I am." I've always taught my daughters that the two most powerful words in the human language are *I am*: yo soy, es sou, Nina, je suis, Em-na, wo shi. Whatever you put after those words is what you will align your mind, heart, and soul to be. So when you capture the virtue on the Post-it, begin with the two words "I am": "I am loyal." "I am a leader." "I am courageous."

It is imperative that you constantly speak positive words of affirmation over yourself. If not, you run the risk of opening the door for someone to speak a negative word, an unGodly word of defeat and not victory. A word of being a victim and not a victor. I believe in using the tangible to help us remember the intangible and achieve the impossible. You see a thing, you remember a thing, and you do a thing! Let these Post-its be constant reminders of your life's purpose and of achieving the impossible. Personally, I've always found the impossible far more fascinating.

PRAYER: OUR CONVERSATIONS WITH GOD

Prayer is our special time to commune with God. Converse with Him for direction and understanding and to gain comfort in what is happening in our lives around us. These conversations with God will erase the worry and allow grace to flow. Oftentimes our lives can be in such turmoil that it can cause us to be mute during prayer time. We are in such despair that we are unable to find the words to articulate what we are feeling and what to ask of our Lord. When you reach these times, just recite the Lord's prayer (Matthew 6:9–13, KJV).

The Lord's Prayer

Our Father who art in heaven, hallowed be Thy name.
(What you are saying: God is my Father. His name is the most Holy of names.)

Thy kingdom come, Thy will be done, on earth as it is in heaven.
(What you are saying: He is still on the throne and in control.)

Give us today our daily bread.
(What you are saying: He always gives me enough to make it through the day. I will focus on what is in front of me and not what is behind or ahead of me.)

And forgive us our debts, as we also have forgiven our debtors.
(What you are saying: I'm letting go of all past hurts and those that have hurt me. I must continue to forgive, just as You forgive me each and every day.)

And lead us not into temptation, but deliver us from the evil one.
(What you are saying: Continue to lead me in my deliverance and avoidance of evil.)

For thine is the kingdom, and the power, and the glory, forever, amen.
(What you are saying: You are my everything, You are all-powerful, You alone are my glory.)

WOMEN OF THE BIBLE

The Bible has a wealth of stories that can inspire and uplift us from well over 100 women. The list below includes some of the most notable that we have not explored previously in this book.

Abigail
Wife of Nabal
1 Samuel 25

Adulterous Woman
Saved by Jesus
John 8

Anna
Prophetess of Christ
Luke 2

Apphia
Wife of Philemon
Philemon 2

Athaliah
Queen of Judah
2 Kings 10 -11

Dorcas
Greek Restored to Life
Acts 9

Drusilla
Daughter of Herod
Agrippa I
Acts 24

Elizabeth
Mother of John the
Baptist
Luke 1

Eunice
Mother of Timothy
Acts 16, 2 Timothy 1

Hagar
Handmaid of Abraham
Genesis 16

Peninnah
Wife of Elkanah
1 Samuel 1

Phoebe
Devoted Helper
Romans 16

Possessed Woman
Daughter of Canaan
Matthew 15

Priscilla
Wife of Aquila
Acts 18, Roman 16

Queen of Sheba
Praised Solomon
1 Kings 10

Bathsheba
Wife of Uriah and
David
2 Samuel 11-12

Hannah
Mother of Samuel
1 Samuel 1-2

Rachel
Wife of Jacob
Genesis 29

Bernice
Daughter of Herod
Agrippa I
Acts 25

Jairus's Wife
Mother of Restored
Daughter
Mark 5

Rebekah
Wife of Isaac
Genesis 24

Candance
Queen of Ethiopia
Acts 8

Jezebel
Queen of Israel
1 Kings 9, 16, 18, 19,
21, 22

Salome
Step-daughter of
Herod Antipas
Matthew 14, Mark 6

Chloe
Believer of Christ
1 Corinthians 1

Joanna
Generous Disciple
Luke 8

Sapphira
Wife of Ananias
Acts 5

Claudia
Sincere Supporter
2 Timothy 4

Leah
Wife of Jacob
Genesis 29

Susanna
Generous Disciple
Luke 8

Delilah
Wife of Samson
Judges 16

Lydia
Businesswoman of
Philippi
Acts 16

Tamar
Raped Princess
2 Samuel 13

Dinah
Daughter of Jacob
Genesis 34

Michal
Daughter of Saul
1 Samuel 18

Zipporah
Wife of Moses
Exodus 2,4,18

REFERENCES

1. American Psychological Association, "Stress in America Findings", released November 9, 2010, https://www.apa.org/news/press/releases/stress/2010/national-report.pdf.

2. Jean-Pierre Isbouts, "50 Most Influential Figures of the Bible", *National Geographic*, Special Edition, National Geographic Partners, LLC.

3. Kelly, Rhonda, and Dorothy Patterson. *The Woman's Study Bible*. Nashville: Thomas Nelson Publishers, 1995.

4. MacVean, Mary, "For Many People, Gathering Possessions Is Just the Stuff of Life", released March 21, 2014, https://article.latimes.com/2014/mar/21/health/la-he-keeping-stuff-20140322.

5. Miller, Stephen. *The Complete Guide to the Bible*. Uhrichsville: Barbour Books, 2007.

6. United States Census Bureau, "The Majority of Children Live with Two Parents, Census Bureau Reports", released November 17, 2016, https://www.census.gov/newsroom/press-releases/2016/cb16-192.html.

DEDICATION

As I continued my tour of the MLK national historic site in Atlanta, I entered into the Ebenezer church and sat in the eleventh pew on the left side. I breathed a sigh of relief because I felt at home as I had never felt before. The gospel music of Mahalia Jackson blared through the speakers, and then came the sermons from Dr. Martin Luther King Jr. himself.

I looked into the pulpit and immediately burst into tears. The pulpit reminded me of a life I once lived many years ago—thirty years ago, to be exact. As I looked up, I could see a vision of my grandparents. My grandfather, Solomon Bullard, who was affectionately called "Big Daddy," was in the pulpit preaching. I was behind him in the choir stand, trying to run up to him. My grandmother, Beatrice Bullard, whom I lovingly called "Big Ma," snatched me back and quieted me. She sent me back to my special little stool to sit.

I couldn't have been more than two years old, but I remember this as clearly as if it happened yesterday. Many studies say that most memories for children start after three years of age, but I remember and can feel this instance as clearly as I remember all the other special moments in my life—the birth of my daughters, my wedding, and my graduation.

I also feel this memory like those other special moments. This recollection has allowed me to feel a connection to my grandparents and this brings me to the place I call *home*—my safe place. I thank my grandparents for imparting upon me strength, determination, and a passion for life, as well as loyalty to those I love and the inspiration for those to whom I am endeared.

I strongly believe in how the law of energy conservation connects to everything in the universe and even to who we are from our ancestries. The law states that energy is neither created nor destroyed, but it is passed from one form to the next. The energy and power that was bestowed upon my grandfather and grandmother didn't go away, and it wasn't destroyed when they passed from earth; it was merely passed on to me to continue their legacy. It is my honor and privilege to do so.

The journey of writing this book has brought me closer to the two most influential people in my life. Big Daddy and Big Ma are now departed from this earth but never from my heart. This book is dedicated to them and their greatness.

I am proud to continue my grandfather's legacy of boldness in ministering the Word to others. As for my grandmother, her strength, tenacity, and leadership continue to inspire all of my endeavors. She will always be my muse. I can imagine my grandparents gazing down upon me from heaven shouting, "Look at our girl!"

Selah

www.ingramcontent.com/pod-product-compliance
Lightning Source LLC
LaVergne TN
LVHW051459070426
835507LV00022B/2846